朝花夕拾

DAWN BLOSSOMS PLUCKED AT DUSK

鲁 迅 著

杨宪益
戴乃迭 译

Written by Lu Xun

Translated by
Yang Xianyi and Gladys Yang

外 文 出 版 社

FOREIGN LANGUAGES PRESS

图书在版编目（CIP）数据
朝花夕拾：汉英对照 / 鲁迅 著；杨宪益，戴乃迭 译.
—北京：外文出版社，2000．9
(经典的回声)
ISBN 7-119-02697-6
I. 朝…　II. ① 鲁… ② 杨… ③ 戴…　III. 英语—对照读物，散文—汉、英　IV. H319.4:I
中国版本图书馆 **CIP** 数据核字（**2000**）第 **66876** 号

外文出版社网址:
http://www.flp.com.cn
外文出版社电子信箱:
info@flp.com.cn
sales@flp.com.cn

经典的回声（汉英对照）

朝花夕拾

作　　者　鲁　迅
译　　者　杨宪益 戴乃迭
责任编辑　胡开敏
封面设计　陈　军
印刷监制　张国祥
出版发行　外文出版社
社　　址　北京市百万庄大街 24 号　　邮政编码　100037
电　　话　（010）68320579（总编室）
　　　　　（010）68329514 / 68327211（推广发行部）
印　　刷　三河市三佳印刷装订有限公司
经　　销　新华书店 / 外文书店
开　　本　大 32 开　　字　　数　130 千字
印　　数　8001—13000 册　　印　　张　8.625
版　　次　2001 年 9 月第 1 版第 2 次印刷
装　　别　平装
书　　号　ISBN 7-119-02697-6 / I・674（外）
定　　价　12.80 元

出版前言

本社专事外文图书的编辑出版，几十年来用英文翻译出版了大量的中国文学作品和文化典籍，上自先秦，下迄现当代，力求全面而准确地反映中国文学及中国文化的基本面貌和灿烂成就。这些英译图书均取自相关领域著名的、权威的作品，英译则出自国内外译界名家。每本图书的编选、翻译过程均极其审慎严肃，精雕细琢，中文作品及相应的英译版本均堪称经典。

我们意识到，这些英译精品，不单有对外译介的意义，而且对国内英文学习者、爱好者及英译工作者，也是极有价值的读本。为此，我们对这些英译精品做了认真的遴选，编排成汉英对照的形式，陆续推出，以飨读者。

外文出版社

Publisher's Note

Foreign Languages Press is dedicated to the editing, translating and publishing of books in foreign languages. Over the past several decades it has published, in English, a great number of China's classics and records as well as literary works from the Qin down to modern times, in the aim to fully display the best part of the Chinese culture and its achievements. These books in the original are famous and authoritative in their respective fields, and their English translations are masterworks produced by notable translators both at home and abroad. Each book is carefully compiled and translated with minute precision. Consequently, the English versions as well as their Chinese originals may both be rated as classics.

It is generally considered that these English translations are not only significant for introducing China to the outside world but also useful reading materials for domestic English learners and translators. For this reason, we have carefully selected some of these books, and will publish them successively in Chinese-English bilingual form.

Foreign Languages Press

目　次
CONTENTS

《朝花夕拾》原版封面

The original cover of *Dawn Blossoms Plucked at Dusk*

小　引

我常想在纷扰中寻出一点闲静来，然而委实不容易。目前是这么离奇，心里是这么芜杂。一个人做到只剩了回忆的时候，生涯大概总要算是无聊了罢，但有时竟会连回忆也没有。中国的做文章有轨范，世事也仍然是螺旋。前几天我离开中山大学的时候，便想起四个月以前的离开厦门大学；听到飞机在头上鸣叫，竟记得了一年前在北京城上日日旋绕的飞机。我那时还做了一篇短文，叫做《一觉》。现在是，连这"一觉"也没有了。

广州的天气热得真早，夕阳从西窗射入，逼得人只能勉强穿一件单衣。书桌上的一盆"水横枝"，是我先前没有见过的：就是一段树，只要浸在水中，枝叶便青葱得可爱。看看绿叶，编编旧稿，

Preface

I often hanker after a little peace and respite from confusion, but it is really hard to come by. The present is so bizarre and my state of mind so confused. When a man reaches the stage when all that remains to him is memories, his life should probably count as futile enough, yet sometimes even memories may be lacking. In China there are rules for writing, and worldly affairs still move in a tortuous course. A few days ago when I left Sun Yat-sen University, I rembered how I left Amoy University four months ago; and the drone of planes overhead reminded me of the planes which, a year ago, had circled daily over Peking. At that time I wrote a short essay called "The Awakening." Today, even this fails to "awaken" me.

It certainly grows hot early in Guangzhou; the rays of the setting sun shining through the west window force one to wear nothing but a shirt at most. The "water-bough" in a basin on my desk is something quite new to me, a lopped-off bough which, immersed in water, will put out lovely green leaves. Looking at these green leaves and editing some old manuscripts means that I am doing something, I

总算也在做一点事。做着这等事,真是虽生之日,犹死之年,很可以驱除炎热的。

前天,已将《野草》编定了;这回便轮到陆续载在《莽原》上的《旧事重提》,我还替他改了一个名称:《朝花夕拾》。带露折花,色香自然要好得多,但是我不能够。便是现在心目中的离奇和芜杂,我也还不能使他即刻幻化,转成离奇和芜杂的文章。或者,他日仰看流云时,会在我的眼前一闪烁罢。

我有一时,曾经屡次忆起儿时在故乡所吃的蔬果:菱角、罗汉豆、茭白、香瓜。凡这些,都是极其鲜美可口的;都曾是使我思乡的蛊惑。后来,我在久别之后尝到了,也不过如此;惟独在记忆上,还有旧来的意味留存。他们也许要哄骗我一生,使我时时反顾。

这十篇就是从记忆中抄出来的,与实际容或有些不同,然而我现在只记得是这样。文体大概很杂乱,因为是或作

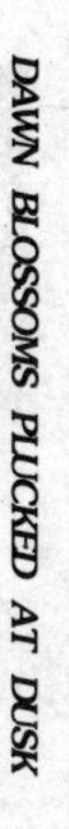

suppose. Doing such trifling things, although really tantamount to death in life, is an excellent way of banishing the heat.

The day before yesterday I finished editing *Wild Grass*; now it is the turn of *Recollections of the past*, serialized in the magazine *Wilderness*, and I have changed its name to *Dawn Blossoms Plucked at Dusk*. Of course flowers plucked with dew on them are much fresher and sweeter, but I was unable to gather these at dawn. Even now I cannot readily transpose my confused thoughts and feelings into bizarre, confused writings. Perhaps some day when I look up at the fleeting clouds, they may flash before my eyes.

For a time I kept recalling the vegetables and fruits I ate as a child in my old home: caltrops, horse-beans, water bamboo shoots, musk-melons. So succulent, so delicious were they all, they beguiled me into longing for my old home. Later, tasting these things again after a protracted absence, I found them nothing special. It was only in retrospect that they retained their old flavour. They may keep on deceiving me my whole life long, making my thoughts turn constantly to the past.

These ten pieces are records transcribed from memory, perhaps deviating somewhat from the facts, but this is just how I remember things today. The writing itself is no doubt a strange hodgepodge, having been jotted down by fits and starts, over a

或辍，经了九个月之多。环境也不一：前两篇写于北京寓所的东壁下；中三篇是流离中所作，地方是医院和木匠房；后五篇却在厦门大学的图书馆的楼上，已经是被学者们挤出集团之后了。

一九二七年五月一月，鲁迅于广州白云楼记。

period of nine months or more. The surroundings differed too: the first two pieces were written by the east wall of my house in Peking; the next three during my wanderings in hospitals and in a carpenter's workshop; the last five on the top floor of the library of Amoy University, when those scholars there had already excluded me from their clique.

Lu Xun

Written in White Cloud Pavilion, Guangzhou
May 1, 1927

狗·猫·鼠

从去年起，仿佛听得有人说我是仇猫的。那根据自然是在我的那一篇《兔和猫》；这是自画招供，当然无话可说，——但倒也毫不介意。一到今年，我可很有点担心了。我是常不免于弄弄笔墨的，写了下来，印了出去，对于有些人似乎总是搔着痒处的时候少，碰着痛处的时候多。万一不谨，甚而至于得罪了名人或名教授，或者更甚而至于得罪了“负有指导青年责任的前辈”之流，可就危险已极。为什么呢？因为这些大脚色是“不好惹”的。怎地“不好惹”呢？就是怕要浑身发热之后，做一封信登在报纸上，广告道：“看哪！狗不是仇猫的么？鲁迅先生却自己承认是仇猫的，而他还说要打‘落水狗’！”这“逻辑”的奥义，即在用我的话，来证明我倒是狗，于是而凡有言说，全都根本推翻，即

Dogs, Cats, and Mice

Since last year I seem to have heard some people calling me a cat-hater. The evidence, naturally, was my tale "Rabbits and Cats," and this being a self-confession there was of course no defence to be made — but that worried me not at all. This year, however, I have begun to feel a little anxious. I cannot help scribbling from time to time, and when what I write is published it seldom scratches certain people where they itch but often strikes them on some sensitive spot. If I am not careful I may even offend celebrities and eminent professors or, worse still, some of the "elders responsible for guiding the youth." And that would be extremely dangerous. Why so? Because these bigwigs are "not to be trifled with." Why are they "not to be trifled with"? Because they may become so incensed that they publish a letter in a paper announcing: "See! Don't dogs hate cats? Mr. Lu Xun himself admits to hating cats yet he also advocates beating 'dogs that have fallen into the water'!" The subtlety of this "logic" lies in its use of words from my own mouth to prove me a dog, from which it follows that any defence I make is completely overturned. Even if I say two

使我说二二得四，三三见九，也没有一字不错。这些既然都错，则绅士口头的二二得七，三三见千等等，自然就不错了。

我于是就间或留心着查考它们成仇的“动机”。这也并非敢妄学现下的学者以动机来褒贬作品的那些时髦，不过想给自己预先洗刷洗刷。据我想，这在动物心理学家，是用不着费什么力气的，可惜我没有这学问。后来，在覃哈特博士（Dr. O. Dahnhardt）的《自然史底国民童话》里，总算发见了那原因了。据说，是这么一回事：动物们因为要商议要事，开了一个会议，鸟、鱼、兽都齐集了，单是缺了象。大家议定，派伙计去迎接它，拈到了当这差使的阄的就是狗。“我怎么找到那象呢？我没有见过它，也和它不认识。”它问。“那容易，”大众说，“它是驼背的。”狗去了，遇见一匹猫，立刻弓起脊梁来，它便招待，同行，将弓着脊梁的猫介绍给大家道：“象在这里！”但是大家都嗤笑它了。从此以后，狗和猫便成了仇家。

日耳曼人走出森林虽然还不很久，

twos make four, three threes make nine, every single word is wrong. And since they are wrong, it follows naturally that those gentlemen are right when they claim that two twos make seven and three threes a thousand.

I tried to investigate the "motive" for their animosity. Far be it from me to ape the fashion of those modern scholars who use motive to belittle a work; I was simply trying to clear myself in advance. To my mind, this would have been an easy matter for an animal psychologist, but unfortunately I lacked that special knowledge. Eventually, however, I discovered the reason in Dr. O. Dähnhardt's *Folk Tales of Natural History* which tells the following tale. The animals called a meeting on important business. All the birds, fish, and beasts assembled with the exception of the elephant. They decided to draw lots to choose one of their number to fetch him, and this task fell to the dog. "How can I find the elephant?" asked the dog. "I've never set eyes on him and have no idea what he looks like." The others replied, "That's easy. He has a humped back." The dog went off and met a cat, which immediately arched its back; so he gave it the message and they went back together. But when he introduced this arched-back cat to the others as the elephant, they simply laughed at him. That was the start of the feud between dogs and cats.

Although it is not very long since the Germans

学术文艺却已经很可观，便是书籍的装潢，玩具的工致，也无不令人心爱。独有这一篇童话却实在不漂亮；结怨也结得没有意思。猫的弓起脊梁，并不是希图冒充，故意摆架子的，其咎却在狗的自己没眼力。然而原因也总可以算作一个原因。我的仇猫，是和这大大两样的。

其实人禽之辨，本不必这样严。在动物界，虽然并不如古人所幻想的那样舒适自由，可是噜苏做作的事总比人间少。它们适性任情，对就对，错就错，不说一句分辩话。虫蛆也许是不干净的，但它们并没有自鸣清高；鸷禽猛兽以较弱的动物为饵，不妨说是凶残的罢，但它们从来就没有竖过"公理""正义"的旗子，使牺牲者直到被吃的时候为止，还是一味佩服赞叹它们。人呢，能直立了，自然是一大进步；能说话了，自然又是一大进步；能写字作文了，自然又是一大进步。然而也就堕落，因为那时也开始了说空话。说空话尚无不可，甚至于连自己也不知道说着违心之论，则对于只能嗥叫的动物，实在免不得"颜厚

came out of their forests, their learning and art are already most impressive; even the binding of their booksand the workmanship of their toys cannot fail to please. But this children's tale is really lacking in charm and offers such a futile reason for a feud. Since the cat did not arch its back to impose on others or give itself airs, the dog is to blame for a lack of acumen. Still, this counts as a reason of a sort. My own dislike of cats is very different.

In fact, no sharp distinction need be drawn between men and beasts. Although the animal kingdom is by no means as free and easy as the ancients imagined, there is less tiresome shamming there than in the world of men. Animals act according to their nature, and whether right or wrong never try to justify their actions. Maggots may not be clean, but neither do they claim to be immaculate. The way vultures and beasts prey on weaker creatures may be dubbed cruel, but they have never hoisted the banners of "justice" and "right" to make their victims admire and praise them right up to the time they are devoured. When man learned to stand upright, that was of course a great step forward. When he learned to write, that was yet another great step forward. But then degeneration set in, because that was the beginning of empty talk. Empty talk is not so bad, but sometimes one may unwittingly say something one doesn't really mean; in which case, compared with inarticulate beasts, men

有忸怩”。假使真有一位一视同仁的造物主，高高在上，那么，对于人类的这些小聪明，也许倒以为多事，正如我们在万生园里，看见猴子翻筋斗，母象请安，虽然往往破颜一笑，但同时也觉得不舒服，甚至于感到悲哀，以为这些多余的聪明，倒不如没有的好罢。然而，既经为人，便也只好“党同伐异”，学着人们的说话，随俗来谈一谈，——辩一辩了。

现在说起我仇猫的原因来，自己觉得是理由充足，而且光明正大的。一、它的性情就和别的猛兽不同，凡捕食雀、鼠，总不肯一口咬死，定要尽情玩弄，放走，又捉住，捉住，又放走，直待自己玩厌了，这才吃下去，颇与人们的幸灾乐祸，慢慢地折磨弱者的坏脾气相同。二、它不是和狮虎同族的么？可是有这么一副媚态！但这也许是限于天分之故罢，假使它的身材比现在大十倍，那就真不知道它所取的是怎么一种态度。然而，这些口实，仿佛又是现在提起笔来的时候添出来的，虽然也像是当时涌上心来的理由。要说得可靠一

should certainly feel ashamed. If there really is a Creator above who considers all creatures as equal, he may think these clever tricks of man rather uncalled for, just as in the zoo the sight of monkeys turning somersaults or female elephants curtseying, although it often raises a laugh, may at the same time make us uncomfortable or even sad, so that we think these uncalled-for tricks might well be dispensed with. However, being men we have to "close ranks against aliens" and try to justify ourselves as men do, according to the fashion of the time.

Now as to my antipathy for cats, I consider that I have ample reason for it, moreover it is open and aboveboard. First, a cat is by nature different from other wild creatures in that whenever it catches a sparrow or mouse instead of killing its victim outright it insists on playing with it, letting it go, catching it again, then letting it go again until tiring of this game it finally eats it. This is very like the bad human propensity for delighting in the misfortunes of others and spinning out their torment. Secondly, although cats belong to the same family as lions and tigers, they are given to such vulgarity! However, this may be owing to their nature. If cats were ten times their present size, there is really no knowing how they would behave. But these arguments may appear thought up at the moment of writing, although I believe they occurred to me earlier on. A sounder explanation perhaps is simply

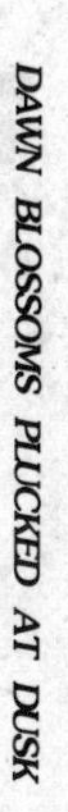

点，或者倒不如说不过因为它们配合时候的嗥叫，手续竟有这么繁重，闹得别人心烦，尤其是夜间要看书，睡觉的时候。当这些时候，我便要用长竹竿去攻击它们。狗们在大道上配合时，常有闲汉拿了木棍痛打；我曾见大勃吕该尔(P. Bruegel d. A)的一张铜版画 Allegorie der Wollust 上，也画着这回事，可见这样的举动，是中外古今一致的。自从那执拗的奥国学者弗罗特(S. Freud)提倡了精神分析说—— Psychoanalysis，听说章士钊先生是译作"心解"的，虽然简古，可是实在难解得很——以来，我们的名人名教授也颇有隐隐约约，检来应用的了，这些事便不免又要归宿到性欲上去。打狗的事我不管，至于我的打猫，却只因为它们嚷嚷，此外并无恶意，我自信我的嫉妒心还没有这么博大，当现下"动辄获咎"之秋，这是不可不预先声明的。例如人们当配合之前，也很有些手续，新的是写情书，少则一束，多则一捆；旧的是什么"问名""纳采"，磕头作

this: their caterwauling when mating has become such an elaborate procedure that it gets on people's nerves, especially at night when one wants to read or sleep. At such times I have to retaliate with a long bamboo pole. When two dogs mate in the street, idlers often belabour them with sticks. I once saw an etching of this by P. Brueghel the Younger entitled *Allegorie der Wollust*, showing that such actions are and always have been common to China and all other countries.

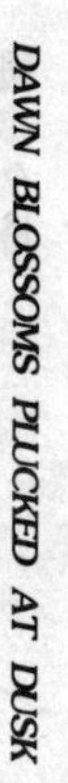

Ever since that eccentric Austrian scholar Sigmund Freud advocated psychoanalysis — which Mr. Zhang Shizhao is said to have translated as "heart examination," a fine, archaic-sounding term but one truly hard to understand — some of our celebrities and eminent professors have make use of it in their insinuations, suggesting that these actions must also perforce be attributed to sexual desire. Now, passing over the business of beating dog to consider my beating of cats, this is solely on account of their caterwauling, quite devoid of malice aforethought, for my jealousy is not yet so inordinate. In these days when one is liable to be blamed at every move, I must proclaim this in advance. For instance, human beings too go through quite a lengthy procedure before mating. The new way is to write love-letters, at least one packet if not a whole sheaf; the old way was to "inquire names," "send betrothal gifts," kowtow and bow. When the Jiang

揖,去年海昌蒋氏在北京举行婚礼,拜来拜去,就十足拜了三天,还印有一本红面子的《婚礼节文》,《序论》里大发议论道:“平心论之,既名为礼,当必繁重。专图简易,何用礼为?……然则世之有志于礼者,可以兴矣!不可退居于礼所不下之庶人矣!”然而我毫不生气,这是因为无须我到场;因此也可见我的仇猫,理由实在简简单单,只为了它们在我的耳朵边尽嚷的缘故。人们的各种礼式,局外人可以不见不闻,我就满不管,但如果当我正要看书或睡觉的时候,有人来勒令朗诵情书,奉陪作揖,那是为自卫起见,还要用长竹竿来抵御的。还有,平素不大交往的人,忽而寄给我一个红帖子,上面印着“为舍妹出阁”,“小儿完姻,”“敬请观礼”或“阖第光临”这些含有“阴险的暗示”的句子,使我不化钱便总觉得有些过意不去的,我也不十分高兴。

但是,这都是近时的话。再一回忆,我的仇猫却远在能够说出这些理由之前,也许是还在十岁上下的时候了。至今还分明记得,那原因是极其简单的:只因为它吃老鼠,——吃了我饲养

family of Haichang had a wedding last year in Peking, they devoted three whole days to ceremonial calls and printed a red-covered Wedding Handbook with apreface in which they expatiated: "Fairly speaking, all rites should be elaborate. If simplicity were our aim, what need would there be for rites?...Thus all who are mindful of rites can rise to action. They should not descend to the level of the common herd who are too low for rites." This did not enrage me, however, because I was not required to attend; and this shows that my hatred of cats is really very easily explained just by that caterwauling so close to my ears. The various rites others indulge in are not the affair of outsiders and don't worry me; but if someone comes and insists on reciting love-letters or bowing and scraping just as I want to read a book or sleep, I have to defend myself with a long bamboo pole too. Then there are people with whom I normally have little to do who suddenly send me a red invitation card to "the nuptials of our younger sister" or "our son's wedding," "craving the honour" of my whole family. I dislike these phrases with their "sinister implications" which embarrass me unless I spend some money.

However, all this belongs to the recent past. Looking further back, my hatred of cats dates from a time long before I could expound these reasons, when I was perhaps ten years old. The reasons I clearly remember was very simple: because cats eat

着的可爱的小小的隐鼠。

听说西洋是不很喜欢黑猫的，不知道可确；但 Edgar Allan Poe 的小说里的黑猫，却实在有点骇人。日本的猫善于成精，传说中的“猫婆”，那食人的惨酷确是更可怕。中国古时候虽然曾有“猫鬼”，近来却很少听到猫的兴妖作怪，似乎古法已经失传，老实起来了。只是我在童年，总觉得它有点妖气，没有什么好感。那是一个我的幼时的夏夜，我躺在一株大桂树下的小板桌上乘凉，祖母摇着芭蕉扇坐在桌旁，给我猜谜，讲故事。忽然，桂树上沙沙地有趾爪的爬搔声，一对闪闪的眼睛在暗中随声而下，使我吃惊，也将祖母讲着的话打断，另讲猫的故事了——

“你知道么？猫是老虎的先生。”她说。“小孩子怎么会知道呢，猫是老虎的师父。老虎本来是什么也不会的，就投到猫的门下来。猫就教给它扑的方法，捉的方法，吃的方法，像自己的捉老鼠一样。这些教完了；老虎想，本领都

mice — ate my beloved small pet mouse.

In the West, it is said, they are not too fond of black cats. I have no idea how correct this is; but the black cat of Edgar Allan Poe's story is certainly rather fearsome. Japanese cats are adept at becoming spirits, and the curelty with which these legendary "cat witches" devour men is even more terrifying. Although China too had "cat spirits" in ancient times, in recent years we very seldom hear of feline black magic; it seems the old craft has died out and they have turned honest. And yet as a child I felt no goodwill towards cats, which to me had something monstrous about them. It so happened that one summer evening during my childhood I was lying on a small table under the cool shade of a large fragrant osmanthus tree while my grandmother, seated beside me waving a plantain fan, regaled me with riddles and stories. Suddenly from the fragrant osmanthus tree we heard a stealthy scratch of claws and two gleaming eyes descended through the darkness. I gave a start, while my grandmother broke off her tale to tell me a different story about cats.

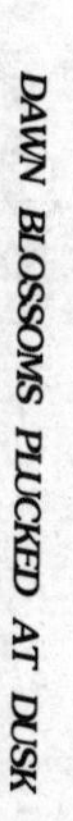

"Did you know that the cat was the tiger's teacher?" she asked. "How could a child know that the cat was once the tiger's master? To start with the tiger couldn't do a thing, so he turned to the cat for help. Then the cat taught him how to pounce on, catch, and eat his prey, the way that it caught rats. After these lessons the tiger thought he had

学到了，谁也比不过它了，只有老师的猫还比自己强，要是杀掉猫，自己便是最强的脚色了。它打定主意，就上前去扑猫。猫是早知道它的来意的，一跳，便上了树，老虎却只能眼睁睁地在树下蹲着。它还没有将一切本领传授完，还没有教给它上树。”

这是侥幸的，我想，幸而老虎很性急，否则从桂树上就会爬下一匹老虎来。然而究竟很怕人，我要进屋子里睡觉去了。夜色更加黯然；桂叶瑟瑟地作响，微风也吹动了，想来草席定已微凉，躺着也不至于烦得翻来复去了。

几百年的老屋中的豆油灯的微光下，是老鼠跳梁的世界，飘忽地走着，吱吱地叫着，那态度往往比“名人名教授”还轩昂。猫是饲养着的，然而吃饭不管事。祖母她们虽然常恨鼠子们啮破了箱柜，偷吃了东西，我却以为这也算不得什么大罪，也和我不相干，况且这类坏事大概是大个子的老鼠做的，决不能诬陷到我所爱的小鼠身上去。这类小

mastered all the skills and no other creature was a match for him except his master the cat. If he killed the cat he would be cock of the walk. He made up his mind to it, and started stalking the cat. But the cat knew what he was up to. With one bound it leaped on to a tree, so that all the tiger could do was squat below glaring up. The cat hadn't taught all its skills: it hadn't taught the tiger to climb trees."

A good thing too, I thought. How lucky that the tiger was so impatient, otherwise a tiger might come crawling down from the fragrant osmanthus tree. Still this was all most alarming, I had better go indoors to sleep. It had grown darker; a breeze had sprung up, rustling the fragrant osmanthus leaves, and the mat on my bed must be cool enough for me to lie quietly without tossing and turning.

A room centuries old, dimly lit by a bean-oil lamp, is the happy hunting-ground of rats who scuttle to and fro squeaking, often giving themselves more arrogant airs than "celebrities and eminent professors." We kept a cat but it didn't earn its keep. Although my grandmother and other grown-ups complained of the way the rats gnawed through chests and stole food, that was no great crime in my eyes, and no business of mine; besides it was no doubt the big rats who were to blame for these misdeeds, and I would not have them slanderously imputed to my pet mouse. My type of mouse, no

鼠大抵在地上走动，只有拇指那么大，也不很畏惧人，我们那里叫它“隐鼠”，与专住在屋上的伟大者是两种。我的床前就帖着两张花纸，一是“八戒招赘”，满纸长嘴大耳，我以为不甚雅观；别的一张“老鼠成亲”却可爱，自新郎、新妇以至傧相、宾客、执事，没有一个不是尖腮细腿，像煞读书人的，但穿的都是红衫绿裤。我想，能举办这样大仪式的，一定只有我所喜欢的那些隐鼠。现在是粗俗了，在路上遇见人类的迎娶仪仗，也不过当作性交的广告看，不甚留心；但那时的想看“老鼠成亲”的仪式，却极其神往，即使像海昌蒋氏似的连拜三夜，怕也未必会看得心烦。正月十四的夜，是我不肯轻易便睡，等候它们的仪仗从床下出来的夜。然而仍然只看见几个光着身子的隐鼠在地面游行，不像正在办着喜事。直到我熬不住了，快

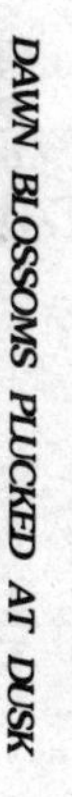

larger than a thumb, mostly scurried about the floor and was not too afraid of people. The local name for them was *yinshu*, and they were a different species from the monsters who lived in the roof. In front of my bed were pasted two coloured woodcuts. One, "The Marriage of Pigsy," consisted almost entirely of long snouts and large ears, and I didn't think much of it. The other, "The mouse's Wedding," was quite charming. Every single mouse in it, from the bridegroom and bride down to the best man, bridesmaids, guests and attendants, had the high cheekbones and slender legs of scholars, although they wore red jackets and green trousers. To my mind, these beloved mice of mine were the only ones capable of conducing such an elaborate ceremony. Nowadays, things are cruder. When I meet a wedding procession in the street, I simply view it as an advertisement for sexual intercourse and pay scant attention. At that time, however, my longing to see a "mouse's wedding" was so strong that I doubt whether it would have exhausted my patience even if the ceremonies had continued for three nights, as in the case of the Jiang family of Haichang. On the eve of the Lantern Festival I was always reluctant to go to sleep as I waited for that procession to emerge from under my bed. But all I saw were the same few mice wearing no clothes and parading the floor as usual, not attending any wedding apparently. When I would hold out no longer I

快睡去，一睁眼却已经天明，到了灯节了。也许鼠族的婚仪，不但不分请帖，来收罗贺礼，虽是真的“观礼”，也绝对不欢迎的罢，我想，这是它们向来的习惯，无法抗议的。

老鼠的大敌其实并不是猫。春后，你听到它“咋！咋咋咋咋！”地叫着，大家称为“老鼠数铜钱”的，便知道它的可怕的屠伯已经光降了。这声音是表现绝望的惊恐的，虽然遇见猫，还不至于这样叫。猫自然也可怕，但老鼠只要窜进一个小洞去，它也就奈何不得，逃命的机会还很多。独有那可怕的屠伯——蛇，身体是细长的，圆径和鼠子差不多，凡鼠子能到的地方，它也能到，追逐的时间也格外长，而且万难幸免，当“数钱”的时候，大概是已经没有第二步办法的了。

有一回，我就听得一间空屋里有着这种“数钱”的声音，推门进去，一条蛇伏在横梁上，看地上，躺着一匹隐鼠，口角流血，但两胁还是一起一落的。取来给躺在一个纸盒子里，大半天，竟醒过来了，渐渐地能够饮食，行走，到第二

fell into a disappointed sleep, and when I opened my eyes again another day had dawned — the Lantern Festival. Perhaps when mice marry they do not issue invitations angling for congratulatory gifts, nor even welcome people really eager to watch. This I imagine has always been their way and to protest is useless.

As a matter of fact the great enemy of mice is not the cat. At the end of spring if you hear the squeaking described as "mice counting coppers" you will know that the butcher of rats has appeared on the scene. This sound, expressing the panic of despair, is not caused by confrontation with a cat. Although a cat is frightening, mice need only dart into a small hole to render it powerless. They have many chances to escape. Only that baneful butcher the snake, long, thin and about the same in circumference as a mouse, can go wherever mice go and is so tenacious in pursuit that few mice escape from it. By the time one hears the "counting of coppers," the mouse is probably doomed.

Once I heard the "counting of coppers" from an empty room. When I opened the door and went in there was a snake on the beam. Lying on the floor I saw a mouse with blood trickling from one corner of its mouth, but still breathing. I picked it up and put it in a cardboard box where after a long time it came to. By degrees it was able to eat, drink and crawl about; and by the next day it

日,似乎就复了原,但是不逃走。放在地上,也时时跑到人面前来,而且缘腿而上,一直爬到膝髁。给放在饭桌上,便检吃些菜渣,舔舔碗沿;放在我的书桌上,则从容地游行,看见砚台便舔吃了研着的墨汁。这使我非常惊喜了。我听父亲说过的,中国有一种墨猴,只有拇指一般大,全身的毛是漆黑而且发亮的。它睡在笔筒里,一听到磨墨,便跳出来,等着,等到人写完字,套上笔,就舔尽了砚上的余墨,仍旧跳进笔筒里去了。我就极愿意有这样的一个墨猴,可是得不到;问那里有,那里买的呢,谁也不知道。"慰情聊胜无",这隐鼠总可以算是我的墨猴了罢,虽然它舔吃墨汁,并不一定肯等到我写完字。

现在已经记不分明,这样地大约有一两月;有一天,我忽然感到寂寞了,真所谓"若有所失"。我的隐鼠,是常在眼前游行的,或桌上,或地上。而这一日却大半天没有见,大家吃午饭了,也不见它走出来,平时,是一定出现的。我

seemed to have recovered. But it did not run away. When put on the ground it kept running up to people and climbing up their legs, right up to the knee. Placed on the dinning-table, it would eat leftovers and lick the edges of bowls. Put on my desk, it would wander about freely and lick some of the ink being ground on the ink-stone. This amazed and delighted me. I had heard from my father that China had an ink-monkey no bigger than a thumb, covered with shining jet-black fur. It used to sleep in the jar for writing-brushes. At the sound of ink being ground it would jump out and wait. When the scholar had finished writing and put away his brush, it would lick up all the ink left on the ink-stone, then jump back into the brush jar. I longed, in vain, to possess one of these ink-monkeys. When I asked where they lived or where they could be bought, nobody could tell me. Something to give satisfaction is better than nothing. This mouse could count as my ink-monkey, although it did not always wait for me to finish writing before licking up my ink.

My recollection is none too clear, but this must have gone on for a month or two before, one day, I suddenly felt as lonely "as if bereft of something." My mouse was always in my sight running about on the table or on the floor. But today I hadn't seen it for hours. It didn't even come after the midday meal, a time when it normally always put in an ap-

再等着，再等它一半天，然而仍然没有见。

长妈妈，一个一向带领着我的女工，也许是以为我等得太苦了罢，轻轻地来告诉我一句话。这即刻使我愤怒而且悲哀，决心和猫们为敌。她说：隐鼠是昨天晚上被猫吃去了！

当我失掉了所爱的，心中有着空虚时，我要充填以报仇的恶念！

我的报仇，就从家里饲养着的一匹花猫起手，逐渐推广，至于凡所遇见的诸猫。最先不过是追赶，袭击；后来却愈加巧妙了，能飞石击中它们的头，或诱入空屋里面，打得它垂头丧气。这作战继续得颇长久，此后似乎猫都不来近我了。但对于它们纵使怎样战胜，大约也算不得一个英雄；况且中国毕生和猫打仗的人也未必多，所以一切韬略、战绩，还是全都省略了罢。

但许多天之后，也许是已经经过了大半年，我竟偶然得到一个意外的消息：那隐鼠其实并非被猫所害，倒是它缘着长妈妈的腿要爬上去，被她一脚踏死了。

这确是先前所没有料想到的。现

pearance. I waited and waited all the rest of the day — still no sign of my mouse.

Mama Chang, my nurse, may have thought this waiting too upsetting for me, for she padded over to whisper something to me which plunged me into a fit of rage and grief and made me vow eternal hatred to cats. She told me that my mouse had been eaten the night before by the cat.

When I lose something I love, it leaves a gap in my heart which I have to fill in with thirst for revenge.

I set about my vengeance with our tabby, extending it gradually to all cats who crossed my path. To start with I just chased and beat them, later I refined on this and learned to hit them on the head with my sling or lure them into an empty room and beat them until they were thoroughly chastened. This feud continued for a very long time until finally it seemed no cats came near me. But triumphing over cats most likely does not make a hero of me; moreover there cannot be too many people in China who keep up a lifelong feud with cats; there I will pass over all my stratagems and exploits.

However, many days later, possibly even more than six months later, I happened to receive some unexpected news. My mouse had not been eaten by a cat — it had been trampled to death by Mama Chang when it tried to run up her leg.

This possibility had never occurred to me. I no

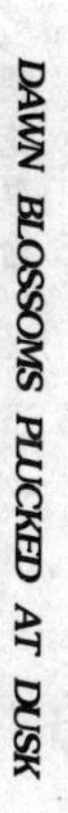

在我已经记不清时是怎样一个感想，但和猫的感情却终于没有融和；到了北京，还因为它伤害了兔的儿女们，便旧隙夹新嫌，使出更辣的辣手。“仇猫”的话柄，也从此传扬开来。然而在现在，这些早已是过去的事了，我已经改变态度，对猫颇为客气，倘其万不得已，则赶走而已，决不打伤它们，更何况杀害。这是我近几年的进步。经验既多，一旦大悟，知道猫的偷鱼肉，拖小鸡，深夜大叫，人们自然十之九是憎恶的，而这憎恶是在猫身上。假如我出而为人们驱除这憎恶，打伤或杀害了它，它便立刻变为可怜，那憎恶倒移在我身上了。所以，目下的办法，是凡遇猫们捣乱，至于有人讨厌时，我便站出去，在门口大声叱曰“嘘！滚！”小小平静，即回书房，这样，就长保着御侮保家的资格。其实这方法，中国的官兵就常在实做的，他们总不肯扫清土匪或扑灭敌人，因为这么一来，就要不被重视，甚至于因失其用

longer remember my immediate reaction, but I was never reconciled to cats. After I came to Peking, the havoc wreaked among my small rabbits by a cat added to my former animosity, and I took sterner measures of reprisal. That gave a handle to those who all call me a cat-hater. But today these are all things of the past andmy attitude to cats has changed to one of extreme politeness. If forced to it I simply drive them away, never beating or hurting them let alone killing them. This is a mark of my progress in recent years. Accumulated experience led me to the sudden realization that nine persons out of ten are naturally disgusted by the way cats steal fish and meat, carry off chickens, or caterwaul late at night, and this disgust is centred on the cats. Should I attempt to rid men of this disgust by beating or killing cats, these would instantly become objects of pity while that disgust would be transferred to me. Accordingly my present method is: whenever I find cats making a nuisance of themselves, I step to my doorway and shout, "Hey! Scram!" When things quieten down a little I return to my study. In this way I preserve my capacity of safeguarding our home against foreign aggression. Actually this method is one commonly practised by officers and soldiers in China, who prefer not to wipe out all brigands or exterminate the enemy completely, for if they did so they would cease to be highly regarded and might even lose their func-

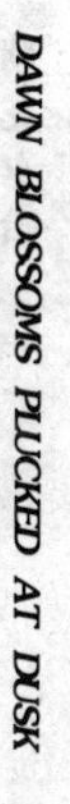

处而被裁汰。我想，如果能将这方法推广应用，我大概也总可望成为所谓“指导青年”的“前辈”的罢，但现下也还未决心实践，正在研究而且推敲。

一九二六年二月二十一日。

tion and their posts. To my mind, if I can get more people to use this tactic, I can hope to become one of the "elders responsible for guiding the youth." But I have not yet decided whether or not to put this into practice. I am still studying and pondering the matter.

February 21, 1926

阿长与《山海经》

长妈妈，已经说过，是一个一向带领着我的女工，说得阔气一点，就是我的保姆。我的母亲和许多别的人都这样称呼她，似乎略带些客气的意思。只有祖母叫她阿长。我平时叫她“阿妈”，连“长”字也不带；但到憎恶她的时候，——例如知道了谋死我那隐鼠的却是她的时候，就叫她阿长。

我们那里没有姓长的；她生得黄胖而矮，“长”也不是形容词。又不是她的名字，记得她自己说过，她的名字是叫作什么姑娘的。什么姑娘，我现在已经忘却了，总之不是长姑娘；也终于不知道她姓什么。记得她也曾告诉过我这个名称的来历：先前的先前，我家有一个女工，身材生得很高大，这就是真阿长。后来她回去了，我那什么姑娘才来

Ah Chang and the *Book of Hills and Seas*

Mama Chang, as I have said elsewhere, was the maid who brought me up or — to give her a grander title — my nanny. That is what my mother and many others called her, for this sounded a little more polite. Only my grandmother call her "Ah Chang." I usually called her "Amah" without even adding the "Chang." But when I was angry with her — upon learnig that she was the one who had killed my mouse, for example — then I also called her "Ah Chang."

We had no one in our parts with the surname Chang; and since she was swarthy, plump and short, "Chang" (long) was not used descriptively either. Nor was it her personal name. I remember she told me her name was Something Girl. What the epithet was I have forgotten, but it certainly was not "Long." And I never knew her surname. I recall her once telling me how she came by the name. Many, many years agao, our family had a very tall maidservant who was the real Ah Chang. Later on, when she left, this Something Girl of mine came to take her place; but because everyone was used to the

补她的缺，然而大家因为叫惯了，没有再改口，于是她从此也就成为长妈妈了。

虽然背地里说人长短不是好事情，但倘使要我说句真心话，我可只得说：我实在不大佩服她。最讨厌的是常喜欢切切察察，向人们低声絮说些什么事。还竖起第二个手指，在空中上下摇动，或者点着对手或自己的鼻尖。我的家里一有些小风波，不知怎的我总疑心和这“切切察察”有些关系。又不许我走动，拔一株草，翻一块石头，就说我顽皮，要告诉我的母亲去了。一到夏天，睡觉时她又伸开两脚两手，在床中间摆成一个“大”字，挤得我没有余地翻身，久睡在一角的席子上，又已经烤得那么热。推她呢，不动；叫她呢，也不闻。

“长妈妈生得那么胖，一定很怕热罢？晚上的睡相，怕不见得很好罢？……”

母亲听到我多回诉苦之后，曾经这样地问过她。我也知道这意思是要她多给我一些空席。她不开口。但到夜里，我热得醒来的时候，却仍然看见满床摆着一个“大”字，一条臂膊还搁在我

name and did not want to change it, from that time on she became Mama Chang too.

Although it is bad to tell tales behind people's backs, if you want me to speak frankly I must admit I did not think much of her. What I most disliked was her habit of gossiping: she would whisper something in people's ears, saw the air with her forefinger, or point to the tip of her hearer's nose or her own. Whenever a minor storm blew up in the house, I could not help suspecting that her tittle-tattle had something to do with it. She restricted my movements too. If I pulled up a weed or turned over a stone, she would say I was naughty and threaten to tell my mother. And in bed during the summer she would stretch out her arms and legs like a huge character 大(*da*), squeezing me so that I had no room to turn over, and my corner of the matting became hot after much lying on. But I could neither push her over, nor could I wake her by shouting.

"You're so plump, Mama Chang, you must find the heat very trying. Isn't that an awkward position for sleeping in?"

My mother put this question after hearing me complaining many times. And I knew it was a hint to my nanny to leave me more space. Ah Chang did not say anything. But that night when the heat woke me up, there was still a big character 大 spread-eagled over the bed, and one of her arms was thrown

的颈子上。我想,这实在是无法可想了。

但是她懂得许多规矩;这些规矩,也大概是我所不耐烦的。一年中最高兴的时节,自然要数除夕了。辞岁之后,从长辈得到压岁钱,红纸包着,放在枕边,只要过一宵,便可以随意使用。睡在枕上,看着红包,想到明天买来的小鼓、刀枪、泥人、糖菩萨……。然而她进来,又将一个福橘放在床头了。

“哥儿,你牢牢记住!”她极其郑重地说。“明天是正月初一,清早一睁开眼睛,第一句话就得对我说,‘阿妈,恭喜恭喜!’记得么?你要记着,这是一年的运气的事情。不许说别的话!说过之后,还得吃一点福橘。”她又拿起那橘子来在我的眼前摇了两摇,“那么,一年到头,顺顺流流……。”

梦里也记得元旦的,第二天醒得特别早,一醒,就要坐起来。她却立刻伸出臂膊,一把将我按住。我惊异地看她

across my neck. It seemed to me there was really no way out.

She was most conventional in many ways, however, though most of her customs made me lose patience. The happiest time of the year was naturally New Year's Eve. After seeing the old year out, I put by my pillow the money wrapped in red paper which the grownups had given me. The next morning I could spend it as I pleased. I lay on my pillow eyeing the red packages, thinking of the small drum, the weapons, the clay figures and the sugar Buddha that I would buy tomorrow. Then she came in and put a Good-Luck Orange at the head of the bed.

"Remember this carefully, son!" she told me earnestly. "Tomorrow's the first day of the first month. When you open your eyes in the morning the first thing you must say is: 'Good luck, Amah!' Remember?" You *must* remember, because this decides the whole year's luck. Don't say anything else, mind! And after you've said that, you must eat a piece of Good-Luck Orange." She picked up the orange and flourished it in front of me. "Then —

> The whole year through
> Luck will follow you!"

Even in my dreams I remembered it was New Year, and the next morning I woke specially early. As soon as I opened my eyes, I wanted to sit up, . But at once she put out an arm to stop me. I looked

时，只见她惶急地看着我。

她又有所要求似的，摇着我的肩。我忽而记得了——

"阿妈，恭喜……。"

"恭喜恭喜！大家恭喜！真聪明！恭喜恭喜！"她于是十分喜欢似的，笑将起来，同时将一点冰冷的东西，塞在我的嘴里。我大吃一惊之后，也就忽而记得，这就是所谓福橘，元旦辟头的磨难，总算已经受完，可以下床玩耍去了。

她教给我的道理还很多，例如说人死了，不该说死掉，必须说"老掉了"；死了人，生了孩子的屋子里，不应该走进去；饭粒落在地上，必须拣起来，最好是吃下去；晒裤子用的竹竿底下，是万不可钻过去的……。此外，现在大抵忘却了，只有元旦的古怪仪式记得最清楚。总之：都是些烦琐之至，至今想起来还觉得非常麻烦的事情。

然而我有一时也对她发生过空前的敬意。她常常对我讲"长毛"。她之所谓"长毛"者，不但洪秀全军，似乎连

at her in surprise, and saw her gazing at me anxiously.

Appealingly, as it were, she shook my shoulder. And suddenly I remembered.

"Good luck, Amah."

"Good luck! Good luck to us every one! Clever boy! Good luck!" Absolutely delighted, she laughed as she stuffed something icy cold into my mouth. When I had recovered from the shock, I realized that this must be the Good-Luck Orange. Now that all the ordeals to usher in New Year's Day were safely over, I could get up and play.

She taught me much other lore as well. For instance, if someone died, you should not say he was dead but "he has passed away." You should not enter a room where someone had died or a child had been born. If a grain of rice fell to the ground, you should pick it up, and the best thing was to eat it. On no account must you walk under the bamboo pole on which trousers or pants were hanging out to dry.... There was more, but I have forgotten most of it; and what I remember most clearly are the strange New Year rites. In short, these were all such niggling trifles that the thought of them today still makes me lose patience.

On one occasion, though, I felt an unprecedented respect for her. She often told me stories about the Long Hairs. And the Long Hairs she described were not only Hong Xiuquan troops but ap-

后来一切土匪强盗都在内,但除却革命党,因为那时还没有。她说得长毛非常可怕,他们的话就听不懂。她说先前长毛进城的时候,我家全都逃到海边去了,只留一个门房和年老的煮饭老妈子看家。后来长毛果然进门来了,那老妈子便叫他们"大王",—— 据说对长毛就应该这样叫,—— 诉说自己的饥饿。长毛笑道,"那么,这东西就给你吃了罢!"将一个圆圆的东西掷了过来,还带着一条小辫子,正是那门房的头。煮饭老妈子从此就骇破了胆,后来一提起,还是立刻面如土色,自己轻轻地拍着胸脯道:"阿呀,骇死我了,骇死我了……。"

我那时似乎倒并不怕,因为我觉得这些事和我毫不相干的,我不是一个门房。但她大概也即觉到了,说道:"像你似的小孩子,长毛也要掳的,掳去做小长毛。还有好看的姑娘,也要掳。"

peared to include all later bandits and rebels as well, with the exception of the modern revolutionaries, who did not exist then. She described the Long Hairs as most fearful beings who talked in a way that no one could understand. According to her, when the Long Haris entered our city all my family fled to the seaside, leaving just a gatekeeper and an old woman who did the cooking to look after the property. Then, sure enough, a Long Hair came to our house. The old woman called him "Great King" — it seems this was the way to address the Long Hairs — and complained that she was starving.

"In that case," said the Long Hair with a grin, "you can have this to eat!" And he tossed over something round with a small queue still attached to it — it was the gatekeeper's head! The old woman's nerves were never the same again. Whenever people spoke of this later, she would turn the colour of earth and beat her breast. "Aiya!" she would whimper. "It gave me such a turn! Such a turn it gave me...."

I was not afraid, for I felt all this had nothing to do with me — I was not a gatekeeper. But Ah Chang must have guessed my thoughts, for she said:

"The Long Hairs would carry off little boys like you as well, to make little Long Hairs out of them. They carried off pretty girls too."

"那么,你是不要紧的。"我以为她一定最安全了,既不做门房,又不是小孩子,也生得不好看,况且颈子上还有许多灸疮疤。

"那里的话?!"她严肃地说。"我们就没有用处?我们也要被掳去。城外有兵来攻的时候,长毛就叫我们脱下裤子,一排一排地站在城墙上,外面的大炮就放不出来;再要放,就炸了!"

这实在是出于我意想之外的,不能不惊异。我一向只以为她满肚子是麻烦的礼节罢了,却不料她还有这样伟大的神力。从此对于她就有了特别的敬意,似乎实在深不可测;夜间的伸开手脚,占领全床,那当然是情有可原的了,倒应该我退让。

这种敬意,虽然也逐渐淡薄起来,但完全消失,大概是在知道她谋害了我的隐鼠之后。那时就极严重地诘问,而且当面叫她阿长。我想我又不真做小长毛,不去攻城,也不放炮,更不怕炮

"Well, you'd be all right anyway."

I was sure she would have been quite safe, for she was neither a gatekeeper, nor a little boy, nor pretty. In fact, she had several scars on her neck where sores had been cauterized.

"How can you say such a thing?" she demanded sternly. "Were we no use to them then? They would carry us off as well. When government troops came to attack the city, the Long Hairs would make us take off our trousers and stand in a line on the city wall, for then the army's cannon could not be fired. If they fired then, the cannon would burst!"

This was certainly beyond my wildest dreams. I could not but be amazed. I had thought of her as nothing but a repository of irksome conventions, never guessing she had this tremendous spiritual power. After this I felt a special respect for her, for surely she was too deep for me to fathom. If she stretched out her arms and legs at night and occupied the whole bed that was quite understandable. I ought to make room for her.

Although this kind of respect for her wore off by degrees, I believe it did not disappear completely till I discovered it was she who had killed my mouse. I cross-examined her sternly on that occasion, and called her "Ah Chang" to her face. Since I was not a little Long Hair and would not attack a city or let off a cannon, I need not be afraid of the cannon exploding — so why, thought I, need I be

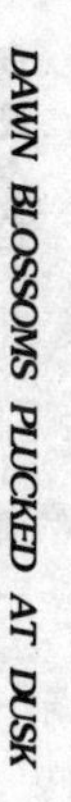

炸,我惧惮她什么呢!

但当我哀悼隐鼠,给它复仇的时候,一面又在渴慕着绘图的《山海经》了。这渴慕是从一个远房的叔祖惹起来的。他是一个胖胖的,和蔼的老人,爱种一点花木,如珠兰茉莉之类,还有极其少见的,据说从北边带回去的马缨花。他的太太却正相反,什么也莫名其妙,曾将晒衣服的竹竿搁在珠兰的枝条上,枝折了,还要愤愤地咒骂道:"死尸!"这老人是个寂寞者,因为无人可谈,就很爱和孩子们往来,有时简直称我们为"小友"。在我们聚族而居的宅子里,只有他书多,而且特别。制艺和试帖诗,自然也是有的;但我却只在他的书斋里,看见过陆玑的《毛诗草木鸟兽虫鱼疏》,还有许多名目很生的书籍。我那时最爱看的是《花镜》,上面有许多图。他说给我听,曾经有过一部绘图的《山海经》,画着人面的兽,九头的蛇,三脚的鸟,生着翅膀的人,没有头而以两乳当作眼睛的怪物,……可惜现在不知道放在那里了。

afraid of her?

But while mourning for my mouse and avenging him, I was also longing for an illustrated copy of the *Book of Hills and Seas*. This longing had been aroused by a distant great-uncle of ours. A fat and kindly old man, he liked to grow plants such as chloranthus, and the rare silk-tree said to have come from the north. His wife was just the reverse: she was an ignoramus as regards flowers. Once she broke a branch of chloranthus by propping the bamboo for hanging our clothes on it; but her only reaction was to swear at the branch for breaking. The old man was a lonely soul with no one to talk to, so he liked children's company and often even called us his "young friends." In the compound where several branches of our clan lived, he was the only one with many books, and unusual ones at that. He had volumes of the essays and poems written for the examinations, of course; but his was the only study where I could find Lu Ji's *Commentaries on the Flora and Fauna in the "Book of Songs,"* and many other strange titles. My favourite in those days was *The Mirror of Flowers* with all its illustrations. He told me there was an illustrated edition of the *Book of Hills and Seas* with pictures of man-faced beasts, nine-headed snakes, three-footed birds, winged men, and headless monsters who used their teats as eyes.... Unfortunately he happened to have mislaid it.

我很愿意看看这样的图画，但不好意思力逼他去寻找，他是很疏懒的。问别人呢，谁也不肯真实地回答我。压岁钱还有几百文，买罢，又没有好机会。有书买的大街离我家远得很，我一年中只能在正月间去玩一趟，那时侯，两家书店都紧紧地关着门。

玩的时侯倒是没有什么的，但一坐下，我就记得绘图的《山海经》。

大概是太过于念念不忘了，连阿长也来问《山海经》是怎么一回事。这是我向来没有和她说过的，我知道她并非学者，说了也无益；但既然来问，也就都对她说了。

过了十多天，或者一个月罢，我还很记得，是她告假回家以后的四五天，她穿着新的蓝布衫回来了，一见面，就将一包书递给我，高兴地说道：——

“哥儿，有画儿的‘三哼经’，我给你买来了！”

我似乎遇着了一个霹雳，全体都震悚起来；赶紧去接过来，打开纸包，是四

Eager as I was to look at pictures of this kind, I did not like to press him to find the book for me. He was very indolent. And none of the people I asked would give me a truthful answer. I had several hundred coppers of New Year money, but no opportunity to buy that book. The main street where books were sold was a long way from our house, and the New Year holiday was the only time in the year when I was able to go there to look around; but during that period the doors of both bookshops were firmly closed.

As long as I was playing it was not so bad, but the moment I sat down I remembered the illustrated *Book of Hills and Seas*.

Probably because I harped on the subject so much, even Ah Chang started asking what this *Book of Hills and Seas* was. I had never mentioned it to her, for I knew she was no scholar, so telling her would serve no purpose. Since she asked me, however, I told her.

About a fortnight or a month later, as I remember, four or five days after she had gone home or leave, she came back wearing a new blue cloth jacket. The moment she saw me she handed me a package.

"Here, son!" she said cheerfully. "I've bought you that *Book of Holy Seas* with pictures."

This was like a thunderbolt. I was struck all of a heap. I hastened to take the package and unwrap

本小小的书，略略一翻，人面的兽，九头的蛇，……果然都在内。

这又使我发生新的敬意了，别人不肯做，或不能做的事，她却能够做成功。她确有伟大的神力。谋害隐鼠的怨恨，从此完全消灭了。

这四本书，乃是我最初得到，最为心爱的宝书。

书的模样，到现在还在眼前。可是从还在眼前的模样来说，却是一部刻印都十分粗拙的本子。纸张很黄；图像也很坏，甚至于几乎全用直线凑合，连动物的眼睛也都是长方形的。但那是我最为心爱的宝书，看起来，确是人面的兽；龙头的蛇；一脚的牛；袋子似的帝江；没有头而“以乳为目，以脐为口”，还要“执干戚而舞”的刑天。

此后我就更其搜集绘图的书，于是有了石印的《尔雅音图》和《毛诗品物图考》，又有了《点石斋丛画》和《诗画舫》。《山海经》也另买了一部石印的，每卷都

the paper. There were four small volumes and, sure enough, when I flipped through the pages, the man-faced beast, the nine-headed snake... all of them were there.

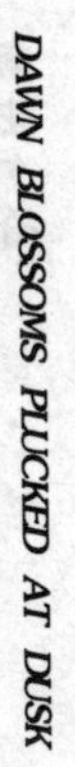

This inspired me with a new respect. What others would not or could not do, she had been able to accomplish. She really did have tremendous spiritual power. My resentment against her for killing my mouse vanished for good and all.

These four volumes were the first I ever possessed, and my most treasured book.

I can still see them today. But now it seems to me that both the printing and the engraving were extremely crude. The paper was yellow and the drawings very poor, consisting almost entirely of straight lines joined together — even the animals' eyes were oblong. Nevertheless this was my most treasured book. There you could really find the man-faced beast, the nine-headed snake, the one-footed ox, the sack-like monster Di Jiang, Xing Tian who had no head but "used his teats as eyes and his navel as mouth" and "danced with spear and shield!"

After this I began seriously collecting illustrated books. I acquired the *Phonetics and Illustrations for "Erh Ya"* and *Illustrations to the "Book of Songs."* I also had the *Paintings Collected by Dianshizhai* and *A Shipload of Painting and Poetry*. I bought another lithographed edition of the *Book of*

有图赞，绿色的画，字是红的，比那木刻的精致得多了。这一部直到前年还在，是缩印的郝懿行疏。木刻的却已经记不清是什么时候失掉了。

我的保姆，长妈妈即阿长，辞了这人世，大概也有了三十年了罢。我终于不知道她的姓名，她的经历；仅知道有一个过继的儿子，她大约是青年守寡的孤孀。

仁厚黑暗的地母呵，愿在你怀里永安她的魂灵！

三月十日。

Hills and Seas too, with illustrations and concluding verses to each chapter. The pictures were green and the characters red — much more handsome than my woodblock edition — and I had this book till the year before last. It was a small edition with Hao Yixing's commentary. As for the woodblock edition, I cannot remember now when that was lost.

My nurse, Mama Chang or Ah Chang, must have departed this life a good thirty years ago. I never found out her name or history. All I know is that she had an adopted son, so she was probably left a widow very early.

Dark, kindly Mother Earth, may her spirit ever rest peacefully in your bosom!

March 10

《二十四孝图》

我总要上下四方寻求，得到一种最黑，最黑，最黑的咒文，先来诅咒一切反对白话，妨害白话者。即使人死了真有灵魂，因这最恶的心，应该堕入地狱，也将决不改悔，总要先来诅咒一切反对白话，妨害白话者。

自从所谓"文学革命"以来，供给孩子的书籍，和欧、美、日本的一比较，虽然很可怜，但总算有图有说，只要能读下去，就可以懂得的了。可是一班别有心肠的人们，便竭力来阻遏它，要使孩子的世界中，没有一丝乐趣。北京现在常用"马虎子"这一句话来恐吓孩子们。或者说，那就是《开河记》上所载的，给隋炀帝开河，蒸死小儿的麻叔谋；正确

The Picture-Book of Twenty-Four Acts of Filial Piety

I shall never cease to search far and wide, high and low, for the blackest, *blackest*, curses for all who oppose and sabotage the use of the vernacular in writing. Even if men's spirits live on after death and I am sent to Hell for such viciousness, I shall certainly not repent but never cease to curse all those who oppose and sabotage the vernacular.

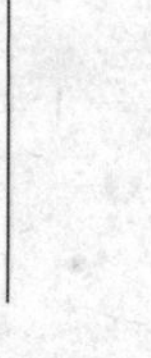

Ever since the so-called "literary revolution," though children's books in China are still most pathetic compared with those in Europe, America and Japan, at least there have been illustrations to go with the text, and as long as children can read they can understand them. However, some people with ulterior motives are doing their utmost to ban these books, in an attempt to make the world of children devoid of every vestige of enjoyment. In Peking today, the term *Ma Huzi* is often used to frighten children. Some say this refers to Ma Shumou who supervised the digging of Grand Canal for Emperor Yang Di of Sui and who, according to the *Record of the Construction of the Canal*, used to steam

地写起来，须是"麻胡子"。那么，这麻叔谋乃是胡人了。但无论他是甚么人，他的吃小孩究竟也还有限，不过尽他的一生。妨害白话者的流毒却甚于洪水猛兽，非常广大，也非常长久，能使全中国化成一个麻胡，凡有孩子都死在他肚子里。

只要对于白话来加以谋害者，都应该灭亡！

这些话，绅士们自然难免要掩住耳朵的，因为就是所谓"跳到半天空，骂得体无完肤，——还不肯罢休。"而且文士们一定也要骂，以为大悖于"文格"，亦即大损于"人格"。岂不是"言者心声也"么？"文"和"人"当然是相关的，虽然人间世本来千奇百怪，教授们中也有"不尊敬"作者的人格而不能"不说他的小说好"的特别种族。但这些我都不管，因为我幸而还没有爬上"象牙之塔"去，正无须怎样小心。倘若无意中竟已撞上了，那就即刻跌下来罢。然而在跌

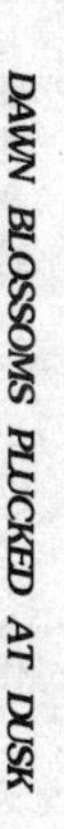

children alive; therefore, properly speaking, the term should mean Ma the Hun. But whether Ma was a Hun or not, there must have been a limit to his eating of children — it must have been confined to his own lifetime. Those, however, who sabotage the use of the vernacular are worse than floods or wild beasts; their pernicious influence is so widespread and so lasting, it can turn the whole of China into a Ma the Hun devouring all children in his murderous maw.

Death to all who conspire to murder the vernacular!

Of course, gentlemen are liable to stop their ears on hearing this, for these are the words of one who "leaps into midair and tears others limb from limb — never ceasing his railing." Men of letters are bound to condemn him too for his flagrant breach of "literary conventions" and consequent loss of "human dignity." For is it not said "Words express what is in the heart"? Of course, "literary style" and "human dignity" are interrelated, although in this world wonders never cease and there is a particular species of professor who "cannot respect" a writer's human dignity yet "has to admit that he writes good short stories." However, this does not worry me, for luckily I have not yet climbed up to any "ivory tower" and therefore need not be on my guard. If by any chance I had scrambled on to one, I should promptly fall off. But in falling, while

下来的中途，当还未到地之前，还要说一遍：——

只要对于白话来加以谋害者，都应该灭亡！

每看见小学生欢天喜地地看着一本粗拙的《儿童世界》之类，另想到别国的儿童用书的精美，自然要觉得中国儿童的可怜。但回忆起我和我的同窗小友的童年，却不能不以为他幸福，给我们的永逝的韶光一个悲哀的吊唁。我们那时有什么可看呢，只要略有图画的本子，就要被塾师，就是当时的“引导青年的前辈”禁止，呵斥，甚而至于打手心。我的小同学因为专读“人之初性本善”读得要枯燥而死了，只好偷偷地翻开第一叶，看那题着“文星高照”四个字的恶鬼一般的魁星像，来满足他幼稚的爱美的天性。昨天看这个，今天也看这个，然而他们的眼睛里还闪出苏醒和欢喜的光辉来。

在书塾以外，禁令可比较的宽了，但这是说自己的事，各人大概不一样。我能在大众面前，冠冕堂皇地阅看的，是《文昌帝君阴骘文图说》和《玉历钞传》，都画着冥冥之中赏善罚恶的故事，

hurtling to theground, I would still repeat:

Death to all who conspire to murder the vernacular!

Whenever I see a schoolchild poring raptly over some crudely printed *Children's World* or the like, I remember what excellent children's books there are in other countries and naturally feel sorry for Chinese children. Yet, when I think back to my classmates'and my own childhood, I cannot but regard today's children as lucky and sadly mourn our youth now gone for ever. What did we have to read? Any book with a few illustrations was banned by our teacher, the "elder" then responsible for "guiding the youth," and we would be reprimanded for reading it or even have our hands caned. When my young classmates got bored to death by reading nothing but "Man is by nature good," they could only turn surreptitiously to the first page to look at the monstrous picture of Kui Xing entitled "The Star of Literature Shines on High," to satisfy their innate childish love for beauty. Day after day this was all they had to look at, yet still their eyes gleamed with growing comprehension and delight.

Outside school, restrictions were relatively less rigid, in my case at any rate, for no doubt it was different for different people. I could read openly in front of others *The God Wenchang Rewards Virtue* and *Records of the Jade Calendar*, both illustrated stories about due deserts being meted out for good

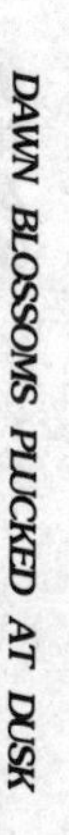

雷公电母站在云中，牛头马面布满地下，不但"跳到半天空"是触犯天条的，即使半语不合，一念偶差，也都得受相当的报应。这所报的也并非"睚眦之怨"，因为那地方是鬼神为君，"公理"作宰，请酒下跪，全都无功，简直是无法可想。在中国的天地间，不但做人，便是做鬼，也艰难极了。然而究竟很有比阳间更好的处所：无所谓"绅士"，也没有"流言"。

阴间，倘要稳妥，是颂扬不得的。尤其是常常好弄笔墨的人，在现在的中国，流言的治下，而又大谈"言行一致"的时候。前车可鉴，听说阿尔志跋绥夫曾答一个少女的质问说，"惟有在人生的事实这本身中寻出欢喜者，可以活下去。倘若在那里什么也不见，他们其实倒不如死。"于是乎有一个叫作密哈罗夫的，寄信嘲骂他道，"……所以我完全诚实地劝你自杀来祸福你自己的生命，因为这第一是合于逻辑，第二是你的言

and evil in the unknown realms, showing the God of Thunder and the Goddess of Lightning in the sky, the Ox-head and Horse-face devils in the nether regions. So not only was it against the rules of Heaven to "leap into midair," even a slip of the tongue, a wrong thought in passing, would meet with the appropriate retribution. Nor would this be a question of "personal resentment," for there gods and ghosts held sway and "justice" governed; thus it would be useless to give a feast or kneel to beg for mercy, there would be simply no way out at all. In the Chinese cosmos it is fearfully difficult to be a man, and equally difficult to be a ghost. Nonetheless there is a better place than earth, a place free from "gentlemen" and "gossip."

To play safe, one must not praise the nether regions. This applies particularly to those who like to flourish a brush-pen in present-day China, under the rule of "gossip" and at a time when "consistency between word and deed" is advocated. We should take warning from previous examples. I have heard that in answer to a girl's question M. Artsybahev once said: Finding happiness in life itself is the only way to go on living; those who can find none would be better dead. Then a fellow called Mikhailov wrote a letter deriding him: "... In this case, in all sincerity I advise you to take your own life; for in the first place this would be logical, in the second it would show that you are as good as

语和行为不至于背驰。”

其实这论法就是谋杀，他就这样地在他的人生中寻出欢喜来。阿尔志跋绥夫只发了一大通牢骚，没有自杀。密哈罗夫先生后来不知道怎样，这一个欢喜失掉了，或者另外又寻到了“什么”了罢。诚然，“这些时候，勇敢，是安稳的；情热，是毫无危险的。”

然而，对于阴间，我终于已经颂扬过了，无法追改；虽有“言行不符”之嫌，但确没有受过阎王或小鬼的半文津贴，则差可以自解。总而言之，还是仍然写下去罢：——

我所看的那些阴间的图画，都是家藏的老书，并非我所专有。我所收得的最先的画图本子，是一位长辈的赠品：《二十四孝图》。这虽然不过薄薄的一本书，但是下图上说，鬼少人多，又为我一人所独有，使我高兴极了。那里面的故事，似乎是谁都知道的；便是不识字的人，例如阿长，也只要一看图画便能够滔滔地讲出这一段的事迹。但是，我

your word."

Actually this argument is an attempt at murder, and that is how Mikhailov found his happiness. Artsybashev simply poured out a stream of complaints but he did not kill himself. What became of Mr. Mikhailov we do not know. This particular happiness slipped through his fingers, but perhaps he found something else in place of it. Certainly "In time like these, courage is the safest course; passion entails no danger."

Still, I have after all already praised Hell, and it is too late to retract. Though this lays me open to the change of "inconsistency in word and action," at least I can defend myself on the strength of the fact that I certainly never accepted half a cent as subsidy from the King of Hell or any lesser devils. So when all's said, I may as well go on writing.

All those pictures I saw of the nether regions were in old books belonging to my family, not in books of my own. The very first picture-book I acquired, a gift from one of my elders, was *The Picture-Book of Twenty-Four Acts of Filial Piety*. Though only a slim volume it had pictures with captions above them, and fewer ghosts than people; moreover it was my personal property, so I was delighted with it. The stories in it were apparently known to all, even to illiterates like Mama Chang, who would launch into a long account after just one glance at a picture. But my initial elation was fol-

于高兴之余，接着就是扫兴，因为我请人讲完了二十四个故事之后，才知道"孝"有如此之难，对于先前痴心妄想，想做孝子的计划，完全绝望了。

"人之初，性本善"么？这并非现在要加研究的问题。但我还依稀记得，我幼小时候实未尝蓄意忤逆，对于父母，倒是极愿意孝顺的。不过年幼无知，只用了私见来解释"孝顺"的做法，以为无非是"听话"，"从命"，以及长大之后，给年老的父母好好地吃饭罢了。自从得了这一本孝子的教科书以后，才知道并不然，而且还要难到几十几百倍。其中自然也有可以勉力仿效的，如"子路负米"，"黄香扇枕"之类。"陆绩怀橘"也并不难，只要有阔人请我吃饭。"鲁迅先生作宾客而怀橘乎？"我便跪答云，"吾母性之所爱，欲归以遗母。"阔人大佩服，于是孝子就做稳了，也非常省事。"哭竹生笋"就可疑，怕我的精诚未必会这样感动天地。但是哭不出笋来，还不

lowed by disappointment, for after asking people to tell me these twenty-four stories, I realized how hard it wasto be "filial." This completely dashed my original foolish hope of becoming a "filial son."

Are men by nature good? This is not a problem we need go into now. Yet I still remember vaguely that as a boy I never really wanted to be unfilial, and was really keen to be a good son to my parents. But I was young and ignorant, and to my mind being "filial" meant nothing more than obedience, carrying out orders and, when I grew up, seeing that my aged parents were well fed. After getting this textbook on filial piety, I realized my error: it was tens or hundreds of times more difficult.

Of couse there were some examples one could emulate, like Zilu's carrying rice or Huang Xiang's fanning the pilow. Nor would it be difficult to hide tangerines in my pocket as Lu Ji had done, so long as some bigwig invited me to a meal. When he asked: "Why are you, a guest, pocketing tangerines, Mr. Lu Xun?" I would kneel to reply: "My mother loves tangerines. I would like to take her back some." Then the bigwig would be filled with admiration and, sure enough, my name would be made as a filial son with a minimum of trouble.

"Weeping to Make the Bamboo Put Out Shoots" presented more of a problem, for my sincerity might not move Heaven and Earth to such an extent. Still, even if my tears failed to produce

过抛脸而已，一到"卧冰求鲤"，可就有性命之虞了。我乡的天气是温和的，严冬中，水面也只结一层薄冰，即使孩子的重量怎样小，躺上去，也一定哗喇一声，冰破落水，鲤鱼还不及游过来。自然，必须不顾性命，这才孝感神明，会有出乎意料之外的奇迹，但那时我还小，实在不明白这些。

其中最使我不解，甚至于发生反感的，是"老莱娱亲"和"郭巨埋儿"两件事。

我至今还记得，一个躺在父母跟前的老头子，一个抱在母亲手上的小孩子，是怎样地使我发生不同的感想呵。他们一手都拿着"摇咕咚"。这玩意儿确是可爱的，北京称为小鼓，盖即鼗也，朱熹曰："鼗，小鼓，两旁有耳；持其柄而摇之，则旁耳还自击，"咕咚咕咚地响起来。然而这东西是不该拿在老莱子手里的，他应该扶一枝拐杖。现在这模样，简直是装佯，侮辱了孩子。我没有

bamboo shoots, it would mean no more than a loss of face, whereas "Lying onIce to Find Carp" could really prove a matter of life and death. The climate in my native parts is so temperate that in the depth of winter only a thin layer of ice forms on the water, but if a child however light lay on the ice — crack! — the ice would be bound to break and I would fall in before any carp had time to swim over to me. Of course, filial piety practised in disregard of one's own life will make God work unlooked-for miracles. But I was too young then to understand such things.

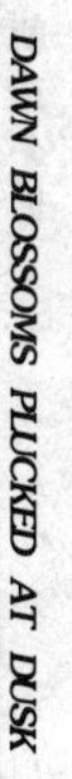

The two stories I found hardest to understand, even reacting with aversion to them, were "Old Lai Zi Amuses His Parents" and "Guo Ju Buries His Son."

I can still remember my different reactions to both: the old man lying on his back before his parents, and the child in his mother's arms. Old man and child alike were holding a rattle. This is really a delightful toy. Known in Peking as a "small drum," the ancients called it *tao*. According to Zhu Xi, "The *tao* is a small drum with ears on both sides which beat against the drum when the handle is shaken." This is what makes a rattle. Still such a thing was out of place in Old Lai Zi's hand, he should instead have been leaning on a stick. His whole behaviour was bogus, an insult to children. I never looked a second time at that picture. As soon

再看第二回，一到这一叶，便急速地翻过去了。

那时的《二十四孝图》，早已不知去向了，目下所有的只是一本日本小田海仙所画的本子，叙老莱子事云："行年七十，言不称老，常著五色斑斓之衣，为婴儿戏于亲侧。又常取水上堂，诈跌仆地，作婴儿啼，以娱亲意。"大约旧本也差不多，而招我反感的便是"诈跌"。无论忤逆，无论孝顺，小孩子多不愿意"诈"作，听故事也不喜欢是谣言，这是凡有稍稍留心儿童心理的都知道的。

然而在较古的书上一查，却还不至于如此虚伪。师觉授《孝子传》云，"老莱子……常著斑斓之衣，为亲取饮，上堂脚跌，恐伤父母之心，僵仆为婴儿啼。"(《太平御览》四百十三引)较之今说，似稍近于人情。不知怎地，后之君子却一定要改得他"诈"起来，心里才能

as I reached that page I would quickly turn over.

I lost track long ago of that *Picture-Book of Twenty-Four Acts of Filial Piety*. The copy now in my possession has illustrations by the Japanese Oda Umisen. The account of Old Lai Zi in this is as follows: "Aged seventy, he did not call himself old but habitually wore motley garments and gambolled like a child before his parents. He also often carried water up to the hall, and would pretend to trip up and fall, then cry like a baby to amuse his parents." The account in my old copy was probably similar. What disgusted me was his *pretending* to trip up. Most small children, whether disobedient or filial, don't like being hypocritical, and when listening to stories they don't like being told lies. Anyone who pays the least attention to child psychology knows this.

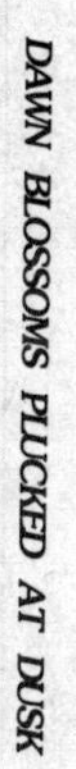

However, if we look up older texts, we find Old Lai Zi was not such a hypocrite. Shi Jueshou's *Accounts of Filial Sons* relates: "Old Lai Zi... habitually wore motley colours to please his parents. Once when mounting the steps to the hall with water fetched for them to drink he fell down and, in order not to distress them, lay there and cried like a baby." (See Book 413 of *The Imperial Encyclopedia of the Taiping Era*.) This sounds more reasonable than the present-day account. Who knows why gentlement of a later age had to change him into a hypocrite before they could rest easy in their minds?

舒服。邓伯道弃子救侄，想来也不过"弃"而已矣，昏妄人也必须说他将儿子捆在树上，使他追不上来才肯歇手。正如将"肉麻当作有趣"一般，以不情为伦纪，诬蔑了古人，教坏了后人。老莱子即是一例，道学先生以为他白璧无瑕时，他却已在孩子的心中死掉了。

至于玩着"摇咕咚"的郭巨的儿子，却实在值得同情。他被抱在他母亲的臂膊上，高高兴兴地笑着；他的父亲却正在掘窟窿，要将他埋掉了。说明云，"汉郭巨家贫，有子三岁，母尝减食与之。巨谓妻曰，贫乏不能供母，子又分母之食。盍埋此子？"但是刘向《孝子传》所说，却又有些不同：巨家是富的，他都给了两弟；孩子是才生的，并没有到三岁。结末又大略相像了，"及掘坑二尺，得黄金一釜，上云：天赐郭巨，官不得取，民不得夺！"

When Deng Bodao abandoned his son to save his nephew, I fancy he simply "abandoned" him, nothing more; but again muddle-headed men had to claimthat, unwilling to let it go at that, he must needs tie his son to a tree to stop the boy from overtaking them. Like "taking delight in what is nauseating," this presentation of inhumanity as morality vilifies the ancients and perverts posterity. Old Lai Zi is a case in point. Regarded by Neo-Confucian gentlemen as an ideal example of impeccable character, in the minds of children he is dead and done for.

But as for Guo Ju's son playing with his rattle, he really deserves compassion. In his mother's arms he is smiling gleefully, yet his father is digging a hole in which to bury him. The caption says: Guo Ju of the Han Dynasty was poor, and his mother denied herself food to give it to his three-year-old son. Guo told his wife: We are too poor to provide well for my mother, and our son is depriving her of food. Should we not bury him? But Liu Xiang's *Lives of Filial Sons* gives another, rather different, version. It says that Guo Ju, a rich man, gave all his property to his two younger brothers; his son was a new-born babe, not a three-year-old. The conclusion is similar: "He dug a pit two feet deep and found a crock of gold on which was written: This is Heaven's reward for Guo Ju. Let no officials confiscate it, no men seize it!"

我最初实在替这孩子捏一把汗，待到掘出黄金一釜，这才觉得轻松。然而我已经不但自己不敢再想做孝子，并且怕我父亲去做孝子了。家景正在坏下去，常听到父母愁柴米；祖母又老了，倘使我的父亲竟学了郭巨，那么，该埋的不正是我么？如果一丝不走样，也掘出一釜黄金来，那自然是如天之福，但是，那时我虽然年纪小，似乎也明白天下未必有这样的巧事。

现在想起来，实在很觉得傻气。这是因为现在已经知道了这些老玩意，本来谁也不实行。整饬伦纪的文电是常有的，却很少见绅士赤条条地躺在冰上面，将军跳下汽车去负米。何况现在早长大了，看过几部古书，买过几本新书，什么《太平御览》啊，《古孝子传》啊，《人口问题》啊，《节制生育》啊，《二十世纪是儿童的世界》啊，可以抵抗被埋的理由多得很。不过彼一时，此一时，彼时

At first I broke into a real cold sweat for that child, not breathing freely again until the crock of gold had been dug up. But by then not only did I no longer aspire to be a filial son myself, I dreaded the thoughtof my father acting as one. At that time our family for tunes were declining, I often heard my parents worrying as to where our next meal was to come from, and my grandmother was old. Suppose my father followed Guo Ju's example, wasn't I the obvious person to be buried? If things worked out exactly as before and he too dug up a crock of gold, naturally that would be happiness great as Heaven; But small as I was at the time I seem to have grasped that, in this world, such a coincidence couldn't be counted on.

Thinking back now, I see what a simpleton I was really. This is because today I understand that no one in fact observes these old fetishes. Despatches and telegrams galore urge us to preserve order and morality, but seldom indeed do we see gentlemen lying naked on the ice or generals alighting from their cars to carry rice. Besides, now that I am a grown man, having read a few old books and bought a few new ones — *The Imperial Encyclopedia of the Taiping Era*, *Lives of Filial Sons of Old*, *The Population Problem*, *Birth Control*, *The Twentieth Century Belongs to the Children* and so forth — I have many arguments to oppose being buried. It is simply that times have changed. In

我委实有点害怕：掘好深坑，不见黄金，连“摇咕咚”一同埋下去，盖上土，踏得实实的，又有什么法子可想呢。我想，事情虽然未必实现，但我从此总怕听到我的父母愁穷，怕看见我的白发的祖母，总觉得她是和我不两立，至少，也是一个和我的生命有些妨碍的人。后来这印象日见其淡了，但总有一些留遗，一直到她去世——这大概是送给《二十四孝图》的儒者所万料不到的罢。

五月十日。

those days I really was rather apprehensive. For if a deep hole was dug but no gold discovered, if rattle and all I was buried and covered with earth, which was then firmly tramped down, what way out could there possibly be? Although I thought this might not necessarily happen, from that time on I dreaded hearing my parents deplore their poverty and dreaded the sight of my white-haired grandmother, feeling that there was no place for the two of us, or at least that she represented a threat to me. Later on this impression faded from day to day, but vestiges of it lingered on until at last she died — this doubtless is something that the Confucian scholar who gave me *The Picture-Book of Twenty-Four Acts of Filial Piety* could never have foreseen.

May 10

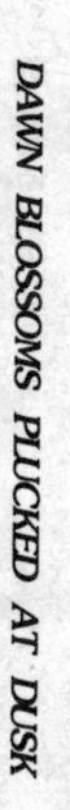

五猖会

孩子们所盼望的，过年过节之外，大概要数迎神赛会的时候了。但我家的所在很偏僻，待到赛会的行列经过时，一定已在下午，仪仗之类，也减而又减，所剩的极其寥寥。往往伸着颈子等候多时，却只见十几个人抬着一个金脸或蓝脸红脸的神像匆匆地跑过去。于是，完了。

我常存着这样的一个希望：这一次所见的赛会，比前一次繁盛些。可是结果总是一个“差不多”；也总是只留下一个纪念品，就是当神像还未抬过之前，化一文钱买下的，用一点烂泥，一点颜色纸，一枝竹签和两三枝鸡毛所做的，吹起来会发出一种刺耳的声音的哨子，叫作“吹都都”的，吡吡地吹它两三天。

现在看看《陶庵梦忆》，觉得那时的赛会，真是豪奢极了，虽然明人的文章，

The Fair of the Five Fierce Gods

In addition to New Year and other festivals, we children looked forward to the temple fairs in honour of certain gods. But because my home was rather out of the way, not till the afternoon did the processions pass our door, by which time the retinue had dwindled away until there was almost nothing left of it. Often, after hours of craning our necks and waiting, all we saw was some dozen men running hastily past carrying an effigy of a god with a golden, blue or crimson face. And that was all.

I always hoped that *this* procession would be bigger and better than the last, but the result was invariably more or less the same. And all I was left with was a souvenir bought for one copper before the god passed by — a whistle make of a bit of clay, a scrap of coloured paper, a split bamboo, and two or three cock's feathers. This whistle, known as a "tootle-toot," produced a piercing blast, and I blew it lustily for two or three days.

Now when I read Zhang Dai's *Reminiscences*, I am struck by the splendour of temple fairs in his time, even if these Ming Dynasty writers do tend to

怕难免有些夸大。因为祷雨而迎龙王，现在也还有的，但办法却已经很简单，不过是十多人盘旋着一条龙，以及村童们扮些海鬼。那时却还要扮故事，而且实在奇拔得可观。他记扮《水浒传》中人物云：“……于是分头四出，寻黑矮汉，寻梢长大汉，寻头陀，寻胖大和尚，寻茁壮妇人，寻姣长妇人，寻青面，寻歪头，寻赤须，寻美髯，寻黑大汉，寻赤脸长须。大索城中；无，则之郭，之村，之山僻，之邻府州县。用重价聘之，得三十六人，梁山泊好汉，个个呵活，臻臻至至，人马称娖而行。……”这样的白描的活古人，谁能不动一看的雅兴呢？可惜这种盛举，早已和明社一同消灭了。

赛会虽然不像现在上海的旗袍，北京的谈国事，为当局所禁止，然而妇孺

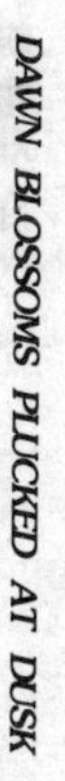

exaggerate. The practice of welcoming the dragon king in praying for rain still continues, but it is very simply done, with only some dozen men carrying a dragon and making it twist and coil, while village boys dress up as sea monsters. In the old days they acted plays, and it was most spectacular. Here is Zhang Dai's description of a pageant with characters from *Shui Hu Zhuan* (*Water Margin*):

"...They went out in all directions to find one fellow who was short and swarthy, another who tall and hefty, a mendicant friar, a fat monk, a stout woman and a slender one. They looked for a pale face too and a head set askew, a red moustache and a handsome beard, a strong dark man and one with ruddy cheeks and a long beard. They searched high and low in the town, and if they failed to find any character they went outside the city walls, to the villages and hamlets in the hills, even to neighbouring prefectures and counties. A high price was paid to the thirty-six men who played the heroes of Liangshan; but each looked his part to the life, and they went out in force on horseback and on foot...."

Who could resist watching such a lifelike pageant of the men and women of days gone by? The pity is that such brave shows disappeared long ago along with the Ming Dynasty.

Though these processions were not prohibited by the authorities — unlike women's long gowns in Shanghai today or the discussion of politics in Pe-

们是不许看的，读书人即所谓士子，也大抵不肯赶去看。只有游手好闲的闲人，这才跑到庙前或衙门前去看热闹；我关于赛会的知识，多半是从他们的叙述上得来的，并非考据家所贵重的“眼学”。然而记得有一回，也亲见过较盛的赛会。开首是一个孩子骑马先来，称为“塘报”；过了许久，“高照”到了，长竹竿揭起一条很长的旗，一个汗流浃背的胖大汉用两手托着；他高兴的时候，就肯将竿头放在头顶或牙齿上，甚而至于鼻尖。其次是所谓“高跷”、“抬阁”、“马头”了；还有扮犯人的，红衣枷锁，内中也有孩子。我那时觉得这些都是有光荣的事业，与闻其事的即全是大有运气的人，——大概羡慕他们的出风头罢。我想，我为什么不生一场重病，使我的母亲也好到庙里去许下一个“扮犯人”的心愿的呢？……然而我到现在终于没有和赛会发生关系过。

　　要到东关看五猖会去了。这是我

king — still, women and children were not allowed to watch them, and educated people or the so-called literati seldom went to look on either. Only layabouts and idlers would gather before the temple or yamen to watch the fun; and since most of my knowledge of these festivites comes from their accounts it is not the firsthand observation so much valued by researchers. I do, however, remember once witnessing a rather fine show myself. First came a boy on horseback called the Announcer. Then, after a considerable interval, the High Pole arrived. This was a great bamboo pole to which a long banner was attached, and it was carried in both hands by a huge fat man dripping with perspiration. When in the mood he would balance the pole on his head or teeth, or even on the tip of his nose. He was followed by stilt-walkers, children on platforms carried by men, and other children on hobby-horses. There were people dressed in red like felons too, loaded with cangues and chains, some of whom were also children. To me each part was glorious and each participant extremely lucky — I very likely envied them this chance to show off. I used to wish I could have some serious illness, so that my mother would go to the temple to promise the god that I would masquerade as a felon.... So far, though, I have failed to have any association with these processions.

Once I was to go to Dongguan Village for the

儿时所罕逢的一件盛事。因为那会是全县中最盛的会,东关又是离我家很远的地方,出城还有六十多里水路,在那里有两座特别的庙。一是梅姑庙,就是《聊斋志异》所记,室女守节,死后成神,却篡取别人的丈夫的;现在神座上确塑着一对少年男女,眉开眼笑,殊与"礼教"有妨。其一便是五猖庙了,名目就奇特。据有考据癖的人说:这就是五通神,然而也并无确据。神像是五个男人,也不见有什么猖獗之状;后面列坐着五位太太,却并不"分坐",远不及北京戏园里界限之谨严。其实呢,这也是殊与"礼教"有妨的,——但他们既然是五猖,便也无法可想,而且自然也就"又作别论"了。

因为东关离城远,大清早大家就起来。昨夜预定好的三道明瓦窗的大船,已经泊在河埠头,船椅、饭菜、茶炊、

Fair of the Five Fierce Gods. This was a great occasion in my childhood, for this fair was the grandest in the whole county and Dongguan Village was very far form my home, more than twenty miles by boat from the town. There were two remarkable temples there. One was the Temple to Lady Mei, the virgin mentioned in the *Tales of Liao Zhai* who remained unmarried after the death of her betrothed and became a goddess after she died, but then appropriated someone else's husband. On the shrine, sure enough, the images of a young man and woman were smiling at each other, counter to all the laws of propriety. The other was the Temple to the Five Fierce Gods, the very name of which was strange enough. According to those with a passion for research, these were the Wu Tong Gods. There is no conclusive proof of this, however. The images were five men who did not look particularly fierce, and behind them sat five wives in a row, this intermingling of sexes falling far short of the strict segregation practised in Peking theatres. In fact, this was counter to all the laws of propriety too; but since these were the Five Fierce Gods, nothing could be done about it. They were obviously an exception to the rule.

Since Dongguan Village was a long way from the town, we all got up at dawn. The big boat with three windows fitted with shell-panes booked the night before was already moored in the harbour,

点心盒子，都在陆续搬下去了。我笑着跳着，催他们要搬得快。忽然，工人的脸色很谨肃了，我知道有些蹊跷，四面一看，父亲就站在我背后。

"去拿你的书来。"他慢慢地说。

这所谓"书"，是指我开蒙时候所读的《鉴略》。因为我再没有第二本了。我们那里上学的岁数是多拣单数的，所以这使我记住我其时是七岁。

我忐忑着，拿了书来了。他使我同坐在堂中央的桌子前，教我一句一句地读下去。我担着心，一句一句地读下去。

两句一行，大约读了二三十行罢，他说：——

"给我读熟。背不出，就不准去看会。"

他说完，便站起来，走进房里去了。

我似乎从头上浇了一盆冷水。但是，有什么法子呢？自然是读着，读着，强记着，——而且要背出来。

粤自盘古，生于太荒，

and to it our menstarted carrying the chairs, food, a stove for brewing tea, and a hamper of cakes. Laughing and skipping, I urged them to get a move on. Suddenly from their respectful expression I knew there was something up. I looked round and saw my father standing behind me.

"Go and fetch your book," he said slowly.

The book he meant was the *Rhymed History* which served as my primer. I had no other book. In our district children started school when their years were odd not even: that is how I know I must have been seven at the time.

With trepidation I fetched the book. He made me sit beside him at the table in the centre of the hall and read to him sentence by sentence. Inwardly quaking, I read to him sentence by sentence.

Two sentences made one line, and I must have read twenty or thirty lines.

"Learn them by heart," he said. "If you cannot recite them correctly, you will not be allowed to go to the fair."

This said, he stood up and walked into his room.

I felt as if someone had doused me with icy water. But what could I do? Naturally I had to read and re-read, and force myself to memorize — I would have to recite it too.

"In the beginning was Pan Gu,
Born of primeval void;

首出御世，肇开混茫。

就是这样的书，我现在只记得前四句，别的都忘却了；那时所强记的二三十行，自然也一齐忘却在里面了。记得那时听人说，读《鉴略》比读《千字文》、《百家姓》有用得多，因为可以知道从古到今的大概。知道从古到今的大概，那当然是很好的，然而我一字也不懂。“粤自盘古”就是“粤自盘古”，读下去，记住它，“粤自盘古”呵！“生于太荒”呵！……

应用的物件已经搬完，家中由忙乱转成静肃了。朝阳照着西墙，天气很清朗。母亲、工人、长妈妈即阿长，都无法营救，只默默地静候着我读熟，而且背出来。在百静中，我似乎头里要伸出许多铁钳，将什么“生于太荒”之流夹住；也听到自己急急诵读的声音发着抖，仿

He was the first to rule the world,
The chaos to divide."

That is the kind of book it was. The first four lines are all I can remember. I have forgotten the rest, including of course the twenty or thirty lines I was forced to memorize that day. I remember hearing it said at the time that studying the *Rhymed History* was more useful than studying the *Thousand Characters* or the *Hundred Surnames*, for from it you could learn the outline of all history past and present. It is naturally a very good thing to know the outline of all history past and present. My trouble was that I couldn't understand a word. "In the beginning was Pan Gu" — to me this was mere gibberish. I read on and learned it by heart.

"In the beginning was Pan Gu,
Born of primeval void...."

Everything needed had been carried to the boat. The noise and bustle at home had turned to silence. The morning sun shone on the western wall. The weather was clear and fine. Mother, the servants, my nanny Mama Chang or Ah Chang — none of them could rescue me. They had to wait in silence till I had learned my lesson and could recite it. In the utter stillness it seemed as if iron pincers would thrust out from my head to seize that "Born of primeval void" and all the other lines. And I could hear my voice quaver as I read desperately

佛深秋的蟋蟀，在夜中鸣叫似的。

他们都等候着；太阳也升得更高了。

我忽然似乎已经很有把握，便即站了起来，拿书走进父亲的书房，一气背将下去，梦似的就背完了。

"不错。去罢。"父亲点着头，说。

大家同时活动起来，脸上都露出笑容，向河埠走去。工人将我高高地抱起，仿佛在祝贺我的成功一般，快步走在最前头。

我却并没有他们那么高兴。开船以后，水路中的风景，盒子里的点心，以及到了东关的五猖会的热闹，对于我似乎都没有什么大意思。

直到现在，别的完全忘却，不留一点痕迹了，只有背诵《鉴略》这一段，却还分明如昨日事。

我至今一想起，还诧异我的父亲何以要在那时候叫我来背书。

五月二十五日。

on, quaver like a cricket's chirping on a late autumn night.

Everybody was waiting. The sun had risen even higher.

Suddenly I felt a surge of confidence. I stood up, picked up the book, and went to my father's study to recite all those lines in one breath. I recited as if in a dream.

"Good. You may go." Father nodded his head as he spoke.

At once everyone sprang into action, breaking into smiles as we set out for the harbour. A servant carried me high as if to congratulate me on my success as he strode ahead of the rest.

I was not as happy as they were, though. After the boat cast off, the riverside scenery, the cakes in the hamper, the bustle of the fair when we reached Dongguan Village — none of these seemed to me very interesting.

Now everything else is forgotten, vanished without a trace. Only my recitation from the *Rhymed History* is as clear in my mind as if it happened yesterday.

Even now, when I think of it, I still wonder why my father made me learn a lesson by heart at a time like that.

May 25

无　常

迎神赛会这一天出巡的神,如果是掌握生杀之权的,——不,这生杀之权四个字不大妥,凡是神,在中国仿佛都有些随意杀人的权柄似的,倒不如说是职掌人民的生死大事的罢,就如城隍和东岳大帝之类。那么,他的卤簿中间就另有一群特别的脚色:鬼卒、鬼王,还有活无常。

这些鬼物们,大概都是由粗人和乡下人扮演的。鬼卒和鬼王是红红绿绿的衣裳,赤着脚;蓝脸,上面又画些鱼鳞,也许是龙鳞或别的什么鳞罢,我不大清楚。鬼卒拿着钢叉,叉环振得琅琅地响,鬼王拿的是一块小小的虎头牌。据传说,鬼王是只用一只脚走路的;但他究竟是乡下人,虽然脸上已经画上些鱼鳞或者别的什么鳞,却仍然只得用了两只脚走路。所以看客对于他们不很

Wu Chang or Life-Is-Transient

If the gods who parade at temple fairs have power of life and death — no, this is wrongly put, for all gods in China seem able to kill men at will — if their task rather, like that of the guardian deity of a city or the Emperor of the East Mountain, is to control human fate, in their retinue you will find some unusual figures: ghostly attendants, the ghostly king, and Wu Chang or Life-Is-Transient.

These spirits are usually impersonated by stout fellows or country folk. The ghostly attendants and their king wear red and green and go barefoot, while on their blue faces are painted fish scales — perhaps the scales of a dragon or some other creature — I am not quite clear on this point. The ghostly attendants carry steel tridents with rings attached which clang when shaken; and the ghostly king carries a small tiger-head tally. According to tradition, the king should walk with one foot; but since after all he is simply a countryman, even though he has painted his face with the scales of a fish or some other creature, he still has to walk with two feet. Hence spectators are not much impressed by these ghosts and pay scant attention to

敬畏，也不大留心，除了念佛老妪和她的孙子们为面面圆到起见，也照例给他们一个"不胜屏营待命之至"的仪节。

至于我们——我相信：我和许多人——所最愿意看的，却在活无常。他不但活泼而诙谐，单是那浑身雪白这一点，在红红绿绿中就有"鹤立鸡群"之概。只要望见一顶白纸的高帽子和他手里的破芭蕉扇的影子，大家就都有些紧张，而且高兴起来了。

人民之于鬼物，惟独与他最为稔熟，也最为亲密，平时也常常可以遇见他。譬如城隍庙或东岳庙中，大殿后面就有一间暗室，叫作"阴司间"，在才可辨色的昏暗中，塑着各种鬼：吊死鬼、跌死鬼、虎伤鬼、科场鬼，……而一进门口所看见的长而白的东西就是他。我虽然也曾瞻仰过一回这"阴司间"，但那时胆子小，没有看明白。听说他一手还拿着铁索，因为他是勾摄生魂的使者。相传樊江东岳庙的"阴司间"的构造，本来是极其特别的：门口是一块活板，人一

them, with the exception of some devout old women and their grand-children, who treat all spirits with proper trepidation and reverence in order that none of them may feel left out.

As for the rest of us — I believe I am speaking for others as well as myself — what we most enjoy watching is Wu Chang. Not only is he lively and full of fun; the mere fact of his being completely in while among that gaudy throng makes him stand out like a stork in a flock of fowls. A distant glimpse of his tall white paper hat and his tattered palm-leaf fan makes everyone feel pleasantly excited.

Of all spirits he is the nearest and dearest to men, and we often come across him. In the temple to the guardian deity of a city or the Emperor of the East Mountain, for example, behind the main hall is a dark room called the Court of Hell; and barely perceptible through the gloom are the images of ghosts: one who died by hanging, one who fell to his death, one who was killed by a tiger, one who expired in the examination cell...but the long white figure you see as you enter is Wu Chang. Though I once paid a visit to the Court of Hell, I was much too timid then to take a good look. I have heard that he carries an iron chain in one hand, because he is the summoner of dead men's spirits. Tradition has that the Court of Hell in the temple of the Emperor of the East Mountain in Fanjiang was strangely constructed with a movable plank just inside the

进门,踏着活板的这一端,塑在那一端的他便扑过来,铁索正套在你脖子上。后来吓死了一个人,钉实了,所以在我幼小的时候,这就已不能动。

倘使要看个分明,那么,《玉历钞传》上就画着他的像,不过《玉历钞传》也有繁简不同的本子的,倘是繁本,就一定有。身上穿的是斩衰凶服,腰间束的是草绳,脚穿草鞋,项挂纸锭;手上是破芭蕉扇、铁索、算盘;肩膀是耸起的,头发却披下来;眉眼的外梢都向下,像一个"八"字。头上一顶长方帽,下大顶小,按比例一算,该有二尺来高罢;在正面,就是遗老遗少们所戴瓜皮小帽的缀一粒珠子或一块宝石的地方,直写着四个字道:"一见有喜"。有一种本子上,却写的是"你也来了"。这四个字,是有时也见于包公殿的扁额上的,至于他的帽上是何人所写,他自己还是阎罗王,我可没有研究出。

threshold. When you entered and stepped on one end of his plank, Wu Chang would fly over from the other end and throw his iron chain neatly round your neck; but after a man had been frightened to death in this way they nailed the plank down. Even in my young days it no longer moved.

If you want to take a good look at him, you will find his picture in the *Records of the Jade Calendar*. It may not be in the abridged version, but in the complete version you are sure to find it. He is wearing deep mourning and straw sandals, with a straw belt round his waist and a string of paper money round his neck. He holds the tattered palm-leaf fan, a chain and an abacus; his shoulders are slightly hunched, his hair is dishevelled; and his eyebrows and eyes tilt down at the sides like the Chinese character 八(*ba*). He wears a peaked, rectangular hat, which, reckoned in proportion to the portrait as a whole, must be about two feet high. In front of the hat, where relicts old and young of the Qing Dynasty would fasten a pearl or jewel on their melon-shaped caps, is the vertical inscription: Good luck to you! According to another version, the words are: So you are here too. This is the same phrase sometimes found on the horizontal tablet over the Court of the Venerable Bao. Whether Wu Chang wrote these words on his hat himself or the King of Hell wrote them for him I have not yet been able to ascertain in the coure of my researches.

《玉历钞传》上还有一种和活无常相对的鬼物，装束也相仿，叫作"死有分"。这在迎神时候也有的，但名称却讹作死无常了，黑脸、黑衣，谁也不爱看。在"阴司间"里也有的，胸口靠着墙壁，阴森森地站着；那才真真是"碰壁"。凡有进去烧香的人们，必须摩一摩他的脊梁，据说可以摆脱了晦气；我小时也曾摩过这脊梁来，然而晦气似乎终于没有脱，——也许那时不摩，现在的晦气还要重罢，这一节也还是没有研究出。

我也没有研究过小乘佛教的经典，但据耳食之谈，则在印度的佛经里，焰摩天是有的，牛首阿旁也有的，都在地狱里做主任。至于勾摄生魂的使者的这无常先生，却似乎于古无征，耳所习闻的只有什么"人生无常"之类的话。大概这意思传到中国之后，人们便将他具象化了。这实在是我们中国人的创作。

然而人们一见他，为什么就都有些紧张，而且高兴起来呢？

凡有一处地方，如果出了文士学者或名流，他将笔头一扭，就很容易变成

In the *Jade Calendar* can also be found Life-Is-Transient's opposite number, a ghost similarly equipped whose name is Death-Is-Predestined. He also appears in temple fairs, where he is wrongly known as Death-Is-Transient. Since his face and clothes are black, nobody cares to look at him. He too appears in the Court of Hell, where he stands facing the wall with a funereal air about him — a genuine case of "knocking against the wall." All who come in to worship and burn incense are supposed to rub his back, and this is said to rid you of bad luck. I rubbed his back too when I was small, but I never seem to have been free of bad luck. Perhaps if I hadn't rubbed it my luck wold have been still worse. This again I have not yet been able to ascertain in the course of my researches.

I have made no study of the canons of Hinayana Buddhism, but I hear that in Indian Buddhist lore you have the god Yama and the ox-headed devil, both of whom reign in hell. As for Mr. Transient, who summons spirits, his origin cannot be traced to ancient times, yet the saying "life is transient" is a common one. I suppose once this concept reached China, it was personified. So Wu Chang is actually a Chinese invention.

But why is everyone pleasantly excited to see him?

When a great scholar or famous man appears anywhere, he has only to flourish his pen to make

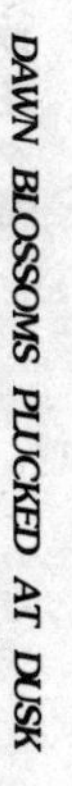

"模范县"。我的故乡,在汉末虽曾经虞仲翔先生揄扬过,但是那究竟太早了,后来到底免不了产生所谓"绍兴师爷",不过也并非男女老小全是"绍兴师爷",别的"下等人"也不少。这些"下等人",要他们发什么"我们现在走的是一条狭窄险阻的小路,左面是一个广漠无际的泥潭,右面也是一片广漠无际的浮砂,前面是遥遥茫茫荫在薄雾的里面的目的地"那样热昏似的妙语,是办不到的,可是在无意中,看得往这"荫在薄雾的里面的目的地"的道路很明白:求婚,结婚,养孩子,死亡。但这自然是专就我的故乡而言,若是"模范县"里的人民,那当然又作别论。他们——敝同乡"下等人"——的许多,活着,苦着,被流言,被反噬,因了积久的经验,知道阳间维持"公理"的只有一个会,而且这会的本身就是"遥遥茫茫",于是乎势不得不发生对于阴间的神往。人是大抵自以为衔些冤抑的;活的"正人君子"们只能骗鸟,若问愚民,他就可以不假思索地回答你:公正的裁判是在阴间!

想到生的乐趣,生固然可以留恋;

the place a "model county." At the end of the Han Dynasty Yu Fan praised my native place; but that after all was too long ago, for later this county gave birth to the notorious "Shaoxing pettifoggers." Of course, not all of us — old and young, men and women — are pettifoggers in Shaoxing. We have quite a few other "low types" too. And you cannot expect these low types to express themselves in such wonderful gibberish as this: "We are traversing a narrow and dangerous path, with a vast and boundless marsh-land on the left and a vast and boundless desert on the right, while our goal in front looms darkly through the mist." Yet in some instinctive way they see their path very clearly to that darkly looming goal: betrothal, marriage, rearing children, and death. Of course, I am speaking here of my native place only. The case must be quite different in model counties. Many of them — I mean the low types of my unworthy county — have lived and suffered, been slandered and blackmailed so long that they know that in this world of men there is only one association which upholds justice, and even that looms darkly; inevitably, then, they look forward to the nether regions. Most people consider themselves unjustly treated. In real life "upright gentlemen" can fool no one. And if you ask ignorant folk they will tell you without reflection: Fair judgements are given in Hell!

Of course, when you think of its pleasures life

但想到生的苦趣，无常也不一定是恶客。无论贵贱，无论贫富，其时都是"一双空手见阎王"，有冤的得伸，有罪的就得罚。然而虽说是"下等人"，也何尝没有反省？自己做了一世人，又怎么样呢？未曾"跳到半天空"么？没有"放冷箭"么？无常的手里就拿着大算盘，你摆尽臭架子也无益。对付别人要滴水不羼的公理，对自己总还不如虽在阴司里也还能够寻到一点私情。然而那又究竟是阴间，阎罗天子、牛首阿旁，还有中国人自己想出来的马面，都是并不兼差，真正主持公理的脚色，虽然他们并没有在报上发表过什么大文章。当还未做鬼之前，有时先不欺心的人们，遥想着将来，就又不能不想在整块的公理中，来寻一点情面的末屑，这时候，我们的活无常先生便见得可亲爱了，利中取大，害中取小，我们的古哲墨翟先生谓之"小取"云。

在庙里泥塑的，在书上墨印的模样上，是看不出他那可爱来的。最好是去看戏。但看普通的戏也不行，必须看"大戏"或者"目连戏"。目连戏的热闹，张岱在《陶庵梦忆》上也曾夸张过，说是

seems worth living; but when you think of its sorrows Wu Chang may not be unwelcome. High or low, rich or poor alike, we must all appear empty-handed beforethe King of Hell, who will right all wrongs and punish evil-doers. Even low types sometimes stop to reflect: What sort of life have I led? Have I "leapt into midair"? Have I "stabbed other people in the back"? In Wu Chang's hand is a big abacus, and no amount of superior airs will do a man any good. We demand undiluted justice from others, yet even in the infernal regions we hope to find some mercy for ourselves. But when all is said, this is hell. And the King of Hell, the ox-headed devil, and the horse-faced devil invented by the Chinese are all working away at one job and honestly administer justice, though they have published no significant articles in the papers. Before becoming ghosts, honest people, when thinking of the future, have to search for fragments of mercy in the sum total of justice and to them Mr. Life-Is-Transient appears rather lovable. "One chooses the greater profit and the lesser evil." This is what our ancient philosopher Mo Di preached.

You cannot see Wu Chang's charm from the clay figure in the temple or the printed picture in the book. The best way is to see him in the opera. And ordinary opera will not do: it must be the Great Drama or Maudgalyayana Drama. Zhang Dai has described in his *Reminiscences* what a fine spectacle

要连演两三天。在我幼小时候可已经不然了,也如大戏一样,始于黄昏,到次日的天明便完结。这都是敬神禳灾的演剧,全本里一定有一个恶人,次日的将近天明便是这恶人的收场的时候,"恶贯满盈",阎王出票来勾摄了,于是乎这活的活无常便在戏台上出现。

我还记得自己坐在这一种戏台下的船上的情形,看客的心情和普通是两样的。平常愈夜深愈懒散,这时却愈起劲。他所戴的纸糊的高帽子,本来是挂在台角上的,这时预先拿进去了;一种特别乐器,也准备使劲地吹。这乐器好像喇叭,细而长,可有七八尺,大约是鬼物所爱听的罢,和鬼无关的时候就不用;吹起来,Nhatu, nhatu, nhatututuu 地响,所以我们叫它"目连嗐头"。

在许多人期待着恶人的没落的凝望中,他出来了,服饰比画上还简单,不拿铁索,也不带算盘,就是雪白的一条

the Maudgalyayana Drama was when it took two to three days to stage the whole play. It was already not nearly so grand in my young days, but just like an ordinary Great Drama, starting in the evening and ending at dawn the next day. Such operas were performed to honour the gods and avert calamities, and each one had an evil-doer who met his end at dawn, when the cup of his sins was full and the King of Hell issued a warrant for his arrest. This was the point at which Wu Chang appeared on the stage.

I remember sitting in a boat below such a stage, with the audience in a different mood from usual. Generally, as the night wore on the crowd grew listless, but at this point they showed fresh interest. Wu Chang's tall paper hat which had been hanging in one corner of the stage was now carried inside, and the musicians took up a peculiar instrument and prepared to blow it lustily. This instrument looked like a trumpet, being long and slender, seven or eight feet in length; and it must have been a favourite with ghosts, for it was played only when there were ghosts on the stage. When you blew it, it blared: *Nhatu*, *nhatu*, *nhatutututuu*! And we called it the Maudgalyayana trumpet.

As the crowd watched eagerly for the fall of the evil-doer, Wu Chang made his appearance. His dress was simpler than in the paintings, and he had neither chain nor abacus; he was simply an uncouth

莽汉，粉面朱唇，眉黑如漆，蹙着，不知道是在笑还是在哭。但他一出台就须打一百零八个嚏，同时也放一百零八个屁，这才自述他的履历。可惜我记不清楚了，其中有一段大概是这样，——

"………

大王出了牌票，叫我去拿隔壁的癞子。
问了起来呢，原来是我堂房的阿侄。
生的是什么病？伤寒，还带痢疾。
看的是什么郎中？下方桥的陈念义la儿子。
开的是怎样的药方？附子、肉桂，外加牛膝。
第一煎吃下去，冷汗发出；
第二煎吃下去，两脚笔直。
我道nga阿嫂哭得悲伤，暂放他还阳半刻。
大王道我是得钱买放，就将我捆打四十！"

这叙述里的"子"字都读作入声 。陈念义是越中的名医，俞仲华曾将他写入《荡寇志》里，拟为神仙；可是一到他的令郎，似乎便不大高明了。la者"的"也；"儿"读若"倪"，倒是古音罢；nga者，"我的"或"我们的"之意也。

他口里的阎罗天子仿佛也不大高明，竟会误解他的人格，——不，鬼格。但连"还阳半刻"都知道，究竟还不失其"聪明

fellow all in white, with white face, red lips and knitted jet-black eyebrow, making it hard to tell whether he was laughing or crying. Upon his entrance he had to sneeze a hundred and eight times and break wind a hundredand eight times before introducing himself. I am sorry I cannot remember all he said, but one passage went something like this:

> ....
> "The King of Hell issued a warrant
> And ordered me to arrest the scabby head next door.
> When I asked who he was, I found he was my cousin's son.
> His illness? Typhoid and dysentery.
> His doctor? The son of Chen Nianyi at Xiafang Bridge.
> His medicine? Aconite, hyssop and cinnamon.
> The first dose brought on a cold sweat,
> At the second his legs stretched stark;
> I said: His mother is weeping piteously,
> Why not restore him to life for a little while?
> But the king accused me of accepting a bribe;
> He had me bound and given forty strokes!..."

Chen Nianyi was a famous doctor in Shaoxing, described as an immortal in the novel *Suppressing the Bandits* by Yu Zhonghua. But his son dose not seem so brilliant in his job.

The King of Hell also does not cut too good a figure in this description, doubting Wu Chang's honesty as he did. Still, the fact that he detected that Wu Chang's nephew had "come to life for a little while" shows him not to fall short of a "just and intelligent god." However, the punishment left our

正直之谓神”。不过这惩罚，却给了我们的活无常以不可磨灭的冤苦的印象，一提起，就使他更加蹙紧双眉，捏定破芭蕉扇，脸向着地，鸭子浮水似的跳舞起来。

Nhatu, nhatu, nhatu-nhatu-nhatututuu!

目连嗐头也冤苦不堪似的吹着。他因此决定了：——

“难是弗放者个！

那怕你，铜墙铁壁！

那怕你，皇亲国戚！

…………”

“难”者，“今”也；“者个”者“的了”之意，词之决也。“虽有忮心，不怨飘瓦”，他现在毫不留情了，然而这是受了阎罗老子的督责之故，不得已也。一切鬼众中，就是他有点人情；我们不变鬼则已，如果要变鬼，自然就只有他可以比较的相亲近。

我至今还确凿记得，在故乡时候，和“下等人”一同，常常这样高兴地正视过这鬼而人，理而情，可怖而可爱的无常；而且欣赏他脸上的哭或笑，口头的硬语与谐谈……。

迎神时候的无常，可和演剧上的又有些不同了。他只有动作，没有言语，

Wu Chang with an ineradicable sense of injustice. As he spoke of it he brows even more and, firmly grasping his tatteredpalm-leaf fan, his head hanging, he started to dance like a duck swimming in the water.

Nhatu, *nhatu*, *hnatu-nhatu-nhatututuu*! The Maudgalyayana trumpet also wailed on in protest against this unendurable wrong.

So Wu Chang made up his mind:

> "Now I shall let no man off,
> Not though he is behind a wall of bronaze or iron,
> Not though he is a kinsman of the emperor! ..."

"Though he has resentment in his heart, he does not blame the unexpected blow." He shows no mercy now. But only against his will, as a result of the King of Hell's reprimand. Of all the ghosts, he is the only one with any human feeling. If we don't become ghosts, well and good; if we do, he will naturally be the only one with whom we can be on relatively close terms.

I still remember distinctly how in my hometown, together with "low types," I often enjoyed watching this ghostly yet human, just yet merciful, intimidating yet lovable Wu Chang. We enjoyed too the grief or laughter on his face, the bravado and the quips that fell from his lips.

The Wu Chang in temple fairs was somewhat different from the one on the stage. He went through certain motions but did not speak, and

跟定了一个捧着一盘饭菜的小丑似的脚色走，他要去吃；他却不给他。另外还加添了两名脚色，就是“正人君子”之所谓“老婆儿女”。凡“下等人”，都有一种通病：常喜欢以己之所欲，施之于人。虽是对于鬼，也不肯给他孤寂，凡有鬼神，大概总要给他们一对一对地配起来。无常也不在例外。所以，一个是漂亮的女人，只是很有些村妇样，大家都称她无常嫂；这样看来，无常是和我们平辈的，无怪他不摆教授先生的架子。一个是小孩子，小高帽，小白衣；虽然小，两肩却已经耸起了，眉目的外梢也向下。这分明是无常少爷了，大家却叫他阿领，对于他似乎都不很表敬意；猜起来，仿佛是无常嫂的前夫之子似的。但不知何以相貌又和无常有这么像？吁！鬼神之事，难言之矣，只得姑且置之弗论。至于无常何以没有亲儿女，到今年可很容易解释了；鬼神能前知，他怕儿女一多，爱说闲话的就要旁敲侧击地锻成他拿卢布，所以不但研究，还早

tagged after a sort of clown who carried a plate of food, wanting to eat but denied food by the latter. There were two additional characters as well — what "upright gentlemen" call the "spouse and offspring." All "low types" have this common failing: they like to do to others as they would be done by. Hence they will not allow even a ghost to be lonely, but pair all ghosts and deities off. And Wu Chang was no exception. His better half was a handsome though rather countrified woman called Sister-in-Law Wu Chang. Judging by this mode of address, Wu Chang must belong to our own generation, so no wonder he gives himself no professorial airs. Then there was a boy in a smaller tall hat and smaller white clothes. Though only a child, his shoulders were already slightly hunched while the tips of his eyebrows drooped. Obviously he was Master Wu Chang, yet everyone called him Ah-ling and showed him little respect — perhaps because he was Sister-in-Law Wu Chang's son by a former husband. In case, though, how could he look so like Wu Chang? Well, the ways of ghosts and spirits are hard to fathom, and we shall simply have to leave it at that. As for why Wu Chang had no children of his own, by this year that is easy to explain. Spirits can foresee the future. He must have feared that if he had many children those liable to gossip would try to prove in devious way that *he* had accepted Russian roubles. So he not only studies birth control

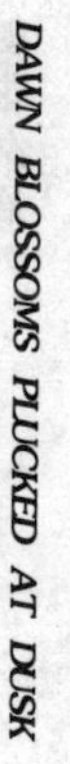

已实行了“节育”了。

这捧着饭菜的一幕，就是“送无常”。因为他是勾魂使者，所以民间凡有一个人死掉之后，就得用酒饭恭送他。至于不给他吃，那是赛会时候的开玩笑，实际上并不然。但是，和无常开玩笑，是大家都有此意的，因为他爽直，爱发议论，有人情，——要寻真实的朋友，倒还是他妥当。

有人说，他是生人走阴，就是原是人，梦中却入冥去当差的，所以很有些人情。我还记得住在离我家不远的小屋子里的一个男人，便自称是“走无常”，门外常常燃着香烛。但我看他脸上的鬼气反而多。莫非入冥做了鬼，倒会增加人气的么？吁！鬼神之事，难言之矣，这也只得姑且置之弗论了。

六月二十三日。

but practises it as well.

The scene with the food is called "The Send Off." Because Wu Chang is the summoner of spirits, the relatives of anyone who dies have to give him a farewell feast. As for not allowing him to eat, this is just a bit of fun in the temple fairs and not the case in fact. But everyone likes to have a bit of fun with Wu Chang, because he is so frank, outspoken and human. If you want a true friend, you will find few better than him.

Some say he is a man who goes to the spirit would, in other words, a human being whose spirit serves in hell while he is asleep. That is why he looks so human. I remember a man who lived in a cottage not far from my home, who claimed to be an "ambulant Wu Chang," outside whose door incense and candles were often burnt. I noticed, though, he had an unusually ghostly expression. Could it be that when he became a ghost in the nether regions his expression became more human? Well, the ways of ghosts and spirits are hard to fathom, and we shall simply have to leave it at that.

June 23

从百草园到三味书屋

我家的后面有一个很大的园，相传叫作百草园。现在是早已并屋子一起卖给朱文公的子孙了，连那最末次的相见也已经隔了七八年，其中似乎确凿只有一些野草；但那时却是我的乐园。

不必说碧绿的菜畦，光滑的石井栏，高大的皂荚树，紫红的桑椹；也不必说鸣蝉在树叶里长吟，肥胖的黄蜂伏在菜花上，轻捷的叫天子(云雀)忽然从草间直窜向云霄里去了。单是周围的短短的泥墙根一带，就有无限趣味。油蛉在这里低唱，蟋蟀们在这里弹琴。翻开断砖来，有时会遇见蜈蚣；还有斑蝥，倘若用手指按住它的脊梁，便会拍的一声，从后窍喷出一阵烟雾。何首乌藤和木莲藤缠络着，木莲有莲房一般的果

From Hundred-Plant Garden to Three-Flavour Study

Behind our house was a great garden known in our family as Hundred-Plant Garden. It has long since been sold, together with the house, to the descendants of Zhu Xi; and the last time I saw it, already seven or eight years ago. I am pretty sure there were only weeds growing there. But in my childhood it was my paradise.

I need not speak of the green vegetable plots, the slippery stone coping round the well, the tall honey-locust tree, or the purple mulberries. Nor need I speak of the long shrilling of the cicadas among the leaves, the fat wasps couched in the flowering rape, or the nimble skylarks who suddenly soared straight up from the grass to the sky. Just the foot of the low mud wall around the garden was a source of unfailing interest. Here field crickets droned away while house crickets chirped merrily. Turning over a broken brick, you might find a centipede. There were stink-beetles as well, and if you pressed a finger on their backs they emitted puffs of vapour from their rear orifices. Milkwort interwove with climbing fig which had fruit shaped like the ca-

实，何首乌有拥肿的根。有人说，何首乌根是有像人形的，吃了便可以成仙，我于是常常拔它起来，牵连不断地拔起来，也曾因此弄坏了泥墙，却从来没有见过有一块根像人样。如果不怕刺，还可以摘到覆盆子，像小珊瑚珠攒成的小球，又酸又甜，色味都比桑椹要好得远。

长的草里是不去的，因为相传这园里有一条很大的赤练蛇。

长妈妈曾经讲给我一个故事听：先前，有一个读书人住在古庙里用功，晚间，在院子里纳凉的时候，突然听到有人在叫他。答应着，四面看时。却见一个美女的脸露在墙头上，向他一笑，隐去了。他很高兴；但竟给那走来夜谈的老和尚识破了机关。说他脸上有些妖气，一定遇见"美女蛇"了；这是人首蛇身的怪物，能唤人名，倘一答应，夜间便要来吃这人的肉的。他自然吓得要死，而那老和尚却道无妨，给他一个小盒

lyx of a lotus, while the milkwort had swollen tubers. Fork said that some of these had human shapes and if you ate them you would become immortal, so I kept on pulling them up. By uprooting one I pulled out those next to it, and in this way destroyed part of the mud wall, but I never found a tuber shaped like a man. If you were not afraid of thorns you could pick raspberries too, like clusters of little coral beads, sweet yet tart, with a much finer colour and flavour than mulberries.

I did not venture into the long grass, because a huge brown snake was said to inhabit the garden.

Mama Chang had told me a story:

Once upon a time a scholar was staying in an old temple to study. One evening while enjoying the cool of the courtyard he heard someone call his name. Responding he looked round and saw, over the wall, the head of a beautiful woman. She smiled, then disappeared. He was very pleased, till the old monk who came to chat with him each evening discovered what had happened. Detecting an evil influence on his face, he declared that the scholar must have seen the Beautiful-Woman Snake — a monster with a human head and snake's body who was able to call a man's name. If he answered, the snake would come that night to devour him.

The scholar was nearly frightened to death, of course; but the old monk told him not to worry and

子，说只要放在枕边，便可高枕而卧。他虽然照样办，却总是睡不着，——当然睡不着的。到半夜，果然来了，沙沙沙！门外像是风雨声。他正抖作一团时，却听得豁的一声，一道金光从枕边飞出，外面便什么声音也没有了，那金光也就飞回来，敛在盒子里。后来呢？后来，老和尚说，这是飞蜈蚣，它能吸蛇的脑髓，美女蛇就被它治死了。

结末的教训是：所以倘有陌生的声音叫你的名字，你万不可答应他。

这故事很使我觉得做人之险，夏夜乘凉，往往有些担心，不敢去看墙上，而且极想得到一盒老和尚那样的飞蜈蚣。走到百草园的草丛旁边时，也常常这样想。但直到现在，总还没有得到，但也没有遇见过赤练蛇和美女蛇。叫我名字的陌生声音自然是常有的，然而都不是美女蛇。

gave him a little box, assuring him that if he put this by his pillow he could go to sleep without fear.

But though the scholar did as he was told, he could not sleep — and that is hardly surprising. At midnight, to be sure, the monster came! There sounded a hissing and rustling, as if of wind and rain, outside the door. Just as he was shaking with fright, however — whizz — a golden ray streaked up from beside his pillow. Then outside the door utter silence fell, and the golden ray flew back once more to its box.

And after that? After that the old monk told him that this was a flying centipede which could suck out the brains of a snake — the Beautiful-Woman Snake had been killed by it.

The moral of this was: If a strange voice calls your name, on no account answer.

This story brought home to me the perils with which human life is fraught. When I sat outside on a summer night I often felt too apprehensive to look at the wall, and longed for a box with a flying centipede in it like the old monk's. This was often in my thoughts when I walked to the edge of the long grass in Hundred-Plant Garden. To this day I have never got hold of such a box, but neither have I encountered the brown snake or Beautiful-Woman Snake. Of course, strange voices often call my name; but they have never proved to belong to Beautiful-woman Snakes.

冬天的百草园比较的无味；雪一下，可就两样了。拍雪人（将自己的全形印在雪上）和塑雪罗汉需要人们鉴赏，这是荒园，人迹罕至，所以不相宜，只好来捕鸟。薄薄的雪，是不行的；总须积雪盖了地面一两天，鸟雀们久已无处觅食的时候才好。扫开一块雪，露出地面，用一枝短棒支起一面大的竹筛来，下面撒些秕谷，棒上系一条长绳，人远远地牵着，看鸟雀下来啄食，走到竹筛底下的时候，将绳子一拉，便罩住了。但所得的是麻雀居多，也有白颊的"张飞鸟"，性子很躁，养不过夜的。

这是闰土的父亲所传授的方法，我却不大能用。明明见它们进去了，拉了绳，跑去一看，却什么都没有，费了半天力，捉住的不过三四只。闰土的父亲是小半天便能捕获几十只，装在叉袋里叫着撞着的。我曾经问他得失的缘由，他只静静地笑道：你太性急，来不及等它走到中间去。

In winter the garden was relatively dull; as soon as it snowed, though, that was a different story. Imprinting a snowman (by pressing your body on the snow) or building snow Buddhas repuired appreciative audiences; and since this was a deserted garden where visitors seldom came, such games were out of place here. I was therefore reduced to catching birds. A light fall of snow would not do: the ground had to be covered for one or two days, so that the birds had gone hungry for some time. You swept a patch clear of snow, propped up a big bamboo sieve on a short stick, sprinkled some rice husks beneath it, then tied a long string to the stick and retired to a distance to hold it, waiting for birds to come. When they hopped under the sieve, you tugged the string and trapped them. Most of those caught were sparrows, but there were white-throated wagtails too, so wild that they died less than a day of captivity.

It was Runtu's father who taught me this method, but I was not adept at it. Birds hopped under my sieve all right, yet when I pulled the string and ran over to look there was usually nothing there, and after long efforts I caught merely three or four. Runtu's father in only half the time coued catch dozens which, stowed in his bag, would cheep and jostle each other. I asked him once the reason for my failure. With a quiet smile he said:

"You're too impatient. You don't wait for them to get to the middle."

我不知道为什么家里的人要将我送进书塾里去了,而且还是全城中称为最严厉的书塾。也许是因为拔何首乌毁了泥墙罢,也许是因为将砖头抛到间壁的梁家去了罢,也许是因为站在石井栏上跳了下来罢,……都无从知道。总而言之:我将不能常到百草园了。Ade,我的蟋蟀们! Ade,我的覆盆子们和木莲们! ……

出门向东,不上半里,走过一道石桥,便是我的先生的家了。从一扇黑油的竹门进去,第三间是书房。中间挂着一块扁道:三味书屋;扁下面是一幅画,画着一只很肥大的梅花鹿伏在古树下。没有孔子牌位,我们便对着那扁和鹿行礼。第一次算是拜孔子,第二次算是拜先生。

第二次行礼时,先生便和蔼地在一旁答礼。他是一个高而瘦的老人,须发都花白了,还戴着大眼镜。我对他很恭敬,因为我早听到,他是本城中极方正,质朴,博学的人。

不知从那里听来的,东方朔也很渊

I don't know why my family decided to send me to school, or why they chose the school reputed to bethe strictest in the town. Perhaps it was because I had spoiled the mud wall by uprooting milkwort, perhaps because I had thrown bricks into the Liangs' courtyard next door, perhaps because I had climbed the well coping to jump off it.... There is no means of knowing. At all events, this meant an end to my frequent visits to Hundred-Plant Garden. Adieu, my crickets! Adieu, my raspberries and climbing figs!

A few hundred yards east of our house, across a stone bridge, was where my teacher lived. You went in through a black-lacquered bamboo gate, and the third room was the classroom. On the central wall hung the inscription Three-Flavour Study, and under this was a painting of a portly fallow deer lying beneath an old tree. In the absence of a tablet to Confucius, we bowed before the inscription and the deer. The first time for Confucius, the second time for our teacher.

When we bowed the second time, our teacher bowed graciously back from the side of the room. A thin, tall old man with a grizzled beard, he wore large spectacles. And I had the greatest respect for him, having heard that he was the most upright, honourable and erudite man in our town.

I forget where it was that I heard that Dongfang Shuo was another erudite scholar who knew of an

博,他认识一种虫,名曰“怪哉”,冤气所化,用酒一浇,就消释了。我很想详细地知道这故事,但阿长是不知道的,因为她毕竟不渊博。现在得到机会了,可以问先生。

“先生,‘怪哉’这虫,是怎么一回事?……”我上了生书,将要退下来的时候,赶忙问。

“不知道!”他似乎很不高兴,脸上还有怒色了。

我才知道做学生是不应该问这些事的,只要读书,因为他是渊博的宿儒,决不至于不知道,所谓不知道者,乃是不愿意说。年纪比我大的人,往往如此,我遇见过好几回了。

我就只读书,正午习字,晚上对课。先生最初这几天对我很严厉,后来却好起来了,不过给我读的书渐渐加多,对课也渐渐地加上字去,从三言到五言,终于到七言。

三味书屋后面也有一个园,虽然小,但在那里也可以爬上花坛去折腊梅

insect called *guai-zai*, the incarnation of some unjustly slain man's ghost, which would vanish if you doused it with wine. I longed to learn the details of this story, butMama Chang could not enlighten me, for she after all was not an erudite scholar. Now my chance had come. I could ask my teacher.

"What is this insect *guai-zai*, sir?" I asked hastily at the end of a new lesson, just before I was dismissed.

"I don't know." He seemed not at all pleased. Indeed, he looked rather angry.

Then I realized that students should not ask questions like this, but concentrate on studying. Being such a learned scholar, of course he must know the answer. When he said he did not know, it meant he would not tell me. Grownups often behaved like this, as I knew from many past experiences.

So I concentrated on studying. At midday I practised calligraphy, in the evening I made couplets. For the first few days the teacher was very stern, later he treated me better; but by degrees he increased my reading assignment and the number of characters in each line of the couplets I was set to write, from three to five, and finally to seven.

There was a garden behind Three-Flavour Study too. Although it was small, you could climb the terrace there to pick winter plum, or search the ground and the fragrant osmanthus tree for the

花，在地上或桂花树上寻蝉蜕。最好的工作是捉了苍蝇喂蚂蚁，静悄悄地没有声音。然而同窗们到园里的太多，太久，可就不行了，先生在书房里便大叫起来：——

“人都到那里去了！”

人们便一个一个陆续走回去；一同回去，也不行的。他有一条戒尺，但是不常用，也有罚跪的规则，但也不常用，普通总不过瞪几眼，大声道：——

“读书！”

于是大家放开喉咙读一阵书，真是人声鼎沸。有念“仁远乎哉我欲仁斯仁至矣”的，有念“笑齿缺曰狗窦大开”的，有念“上九潜龙勿用”的，有念“厥土下上上错厥贡苞茅橘柚”的……。先生自己也念书。后来，我们的声音便低下去，静下去了，只有他还大声朗读着：——

“铁如意，指挥倜傥，一座皆惊呢

moulted skins of cicadas. Best of all was catching flies to feed ants, for that did not make any noise. But it was no use too many of us slipping out into the garden at the same time or staying out too long, for then the teacher would shout from the classroom:

"Where has everybody gone?"

Then everyone would slip back one after the other: it was no use all going back together. He had a ferule which he seldom used, and a method of punishing students by making them kneel which again he seldom used. In general, he simply glared round for a while and shouted:

"Get on with your reading!"

Then all of us would read at the top of our voices, with a roar like a seething cauldron.

We all read from different texts:

"Is humanity far? When I seek it, it is here."

"To mock a toothless man, say: The dog's kennel gapes wide."

"On the upper ninth the dragon hides itself and bides its time."

"Poor soil, with good produce of the inferior sort interspersed with superior produce; its tribute, matting, oranges, pomelos."

....

The teacher read aloud too. Later, our voices grew lower and faded away. He alone went on declaiming as loudly as ever:

"At a sweep of his iron sceptre, all stand

~~~~;金叵罗,颠倒淋漓噫,千杯未醉嗬~~~~……。”

我疑心这是极好的文章,因为读到这里,他总是微笑起来,而且将头仰起,摇着,向后面拗过去,拗过去。

先生读书入神的时候,于我们是很相宜的。有几个便用纸糊的盔甲套在指甲上做戏。我是画画儿,用一种叫作“荆川纸”的,蒙在小说的绣像上一个个描下来,像习字时候的影写一样。读的书多起来,画的画也多起来;书没有读成,画的成绩却不少了,最成片段的是《荡寇志》和《西游记》的绣像,都有一大本。后来,因为要钱用,卖给一个有钱的同窗了。他的父亲是开锡箔店的;听说现在自己已经做了店主,而且快要升到绅士的地位了。这东西早已没有了罢。

九月十八日。
~~~~

amazed.... The golden goblet brims over, but a thousand cups will not intoxicate him...."

I suspected this to be the finest literature, for whenever he reached this passage he always smiled, threw back his head a little and shook it, bending his head further and further back.

When our teacher was completely absorbed in his reading, that was most convenient for us. Some boys would then stage puppet shows with paper helmets on their fingers. I used to draw, using what we called "Jingchuan paper" to trace the illustrations to various novels, just as we traced calligraphy. The more books I read, the more illustrations I traced. I never became a good student but I made not a little progress as an artist, the best sets I copied being two big volumes of illustration, one from *Suppressing the Bandits*, the other from *Pilgrimage to the West*. Later, needing ready money, I sold these to a rich classmate whose father ran a shop selling the tinsel coins used at funerals. I hear he is now the shop manager himself and will soon have risen to the rank of one of the local gentry. Those tracings of mine must have vanished long ago.

September 18

父亲的病

大约十多年前罢，S城中曾经盛传过一个名医的故事：——

他出诊原来是一元四角，特拔十元，深夜加倍，出城又加倍。有一夜，一家城外人家的闺女生急病，来请他了，因为他其时已经阔得不耐烦，便非一百元不去。他们只得都依他。待去时，却只是草草地一看，说道"不要紧的"，开一张方，拿了一百元就走。那病家似乎很有钱，第二天又来请了。他一到门，只见主人笑面承迎，道，"昨晚服了先生的药，好得多了，所以再请你来复诊一

Father's Illness

It is probable over ten years now since this story of a well-known doctor was the talk of the town in S—:

He charged one dollar forty a visit, ten dollars for an emergency call, double the amount for a night call, and double again for a trip outside the city. One night the daughter of a family living outside the city fell dangerously ill. They sent to ask him out there and, because he had more money at the time than he knew what to do with, he refused to go for less than a hundred dollars. They had to agree to this. Once there, though, he simply gave the girl a perfunctory looking over.

"It isn't serious," he said.

Then he made out prescription, took his hundred doolars, and left.

Apparently the patient's family was very rich, for the next day they asked him out there again. The master of the house met him at the door with a smile.

"Yesterday evening we gave her your medicine, Doctor," he said, "and she's much better. So we've asked you to have another look at her."

回。”仍旧引到房里，老妈子便将病人的手拉出帐外来。他一按，冷冰冰的，也没有脉，于是点点头道，“唔，这病我明白了。”从从容容走到桌前，取了药方纸，提笔写道：——

“凭票付英洋壹百元正。”下面是署名，画押。

“先生，这病看来很不轻了，用药怕还得重一点罢。”主人在背后说。

“可以，”他说。于是另开了一张方，——

“凭票付英洋贰百元正。”下面仍是署名，画押。

这样，主人就收了药方，很客气地送他出来了。

我曾经和这名医周旋过两整年，因为他隔日一回，来诊我的父亲的病。那时虽然已经很有名，但还不至于阔得这样不耐烦；可是诊金却已经是一元四角。现在的都市上，诊金一次十元并不算奇，可是那时是一元四角已是巨款，

He took him as before into the bedroom, and a maid drew the patient's hand outside the bed curtain. The doctor placed his fingers on the wrist and found it icy cold, without any pulse.

"Hmm." He nodded. "I understand this illness."

Quite calmly he walked to the table, took out a prescription form, and wrote on it: "Pay the bearer one hundred silver dollars."

Beneath he signed his name and affixed his seal.

"This illness looks rather serious, Doctor," said the master of the house, behind him. "I think the medicine should be a little more potent."

"Very well." said the doctor. And he wrote another prescription: "Pay the bearer two hundred silver dollars."

Beneath he signed his name and affixed his seal again.

This done, the master of the house put away the prescription and saw him politely out.

I had dealings with this famous physician for two whole years, because he came every other day to attend my father. Although by that time very well known, he had not yet more money than he knew what to do with; still, his fee was already one dollar forty a visit. In large towns today a ten-dollar fee is not considered exorbitant; but in those days one dollar forty was a great sum, by no means easy

很不容易张罗的了；又何况是隔日一次。他大概的确有些特别，据舆论说，用药就与众不同。我不知道药品，所觉得的，就是“药引”的难得，新方一换，就得忙一大场。先买药，再寻药引。“生姜”两片，竹叶十片去尖，他是不用的了。起码是芦根，须到河边去掘；一到经霜三年的甘蔗，便至少也得搜寻两三天。可是说也奇怪，大约后来总没有购求不到的。

据舆论说，神妙就在这地方。先前有一个病人，百药无效；待到遇见了什么叶天士先生，只在旧方上加了一味药引：梧桐叶。只一服，便霍然而愈了。“医者，意也。”其时是秋天，而梧桐先知秋气。其先百药不投，今以秋气动之，以气感气，所以……。我虽然并不了然，但也十分佩服，知道凡有灵药，一定

to raise — especially when it fell due every other day.

He probably *was* unique in some respects. It was generally agreed that his prescriptions were unusual. I know nothing about medicine: what struck me was how hard his "adjuvants" were to find. Each new prescription kept me busy for some time. First I had to buy the medicine, then look for the adjuvant. He never used such common ingredients as two slices of fresh ginger, or ten bamboo leaves minus the tips. At best it was reed roots, and I had to go to the river to dig them up; and when it came to sugar-cane which had seen three years of frost, I would have to search for two or three days at the least. But, strange to say, I believe my quest was always successful in the end.

It was generally agreed that herein lay his magic. There once was a patient whom no drugs could cure, but when he met a certain Dr. Ye Tianshi, all this doctor did was to add phoenix-tree leaves as the adjuvant to the old prescription. With only one dose the patient was cured. "Medicine is a matter of the mind." Because it was autumn then, and the phoenix tree is the first to feel the approach of autumn, where all other drugs had failed, Dr. Ye could now use the spirit of autumn. When spirit reacted on spirit, the patient was thus.... Although this was not clear to me, I was thoroughly impressed and realized that all efficacious drugs must

是很不容易得到的，求仙的人，甚至于还要拼了性命，跑进深山里去采呢。

这样有两年，渐渐地熟识，几乎是朋友了。父亲的水肿是逐日利害，将要不能起床；我对于经霜三年的甘蔗之流也逐渐失了信仰，采办药引似乎再没有先前一般踊跃了。正在这时候，他有一天来诊，问过病状，便极其诚恳地说：——

“我所有的学问，都用尽了。这里还有一位陈莲河先生，本领比我高。我荐他来看一看，我可以写一封信。可是，病是不要紧的，不过经他的手，可以格外好得快……。”

这一天似乎大家都有些不欢，仍然由我恭敬地送他上轿。进来时，看见父亲的脸色很异样，和大家谈论，大意是说自己的病大概没有希望的了；他因为看了两年，毫无效验，脸又太熟了，未免有些难以为情，所以等到危急时候，便荐一个生手自代，和自己完全脱了干

be difficult to get. Those who want to become immortals even have to risk their lives to go deep into the mountains to pluck the herb of long life.

After two years of his visits, I gradually came to know this famous physician fairly well; indeed we were almost friends. Father's dropsy grew daily worse, till it looked as if he would have to keep to his bed, and by degrees I lost faith in such remedies as sugar-cane which had seen three years of frost, and was not nearly as zealous as before in finding and preparing adjuvants. One day just at this time, when the doctor called, after inquiring after my father's illness he told us very frankly:

"I've used all the knowledge I have. There is a Dr. Chen Lianhe here, who knows more than I do. I advise you to consult him. I'll write you a letter of introduction. This illness isn't serious, though. It's just that he can cure it much more quickly...."

The whole household seemed rather unhappy that day, but I saw him out as respectfully as ever to his sedan-chair. When I went in again, I found my father looking very put out, talking it over with everyone and declaring that there was probably no hope for him. Because this doctor had treated the illness for two years to no purpose, and knew the patient too well, he could not help feeling rather embarrassed now that things had reached a crisis: that was why he had recommended someone else, washing his hands of the whole affair. But what

系。但另外有什么法子呢？本城的名医，除他之外，实在也只有一个陈莲河了。明天就请陈莲河。

陈莲河的诊金也是一元四角。但前回的名医的脸是圆而胖的，他却长而胖了：这一点颇不同。还有用药也不同。前回的名医是一个人还可以办的，这一回却是一个人有些办不妥帖了，因为他一张药方上，总兼有一种特别的丸散和一种奇特的药引。

芦根和经霜三年的甘蔗，他就从来没有用过。最平常的是"蟋蟀一对"，旁注小字道："要原配，即本在一窠中者。"似乎昆虫也要贞节，续弦或再醮，连做药资格也丧失了。但这差使在我并不为难，走进百草园，十对也容易得，将它们用线一缚，活活地掷入沸汤中完事。然而还有"平地木十株"呢，这可谁也不知道是什么东西了，问药店，问乡下人，问卖草药的，问老年人，问读书人，问木匠，都只是摇摇头，临末才记起了那远

else could we do? It was a fact that the only other well-known doctor in our town was Chen Lianhe. So the next day we engaged his services.

Chen Lianhe's fee was also one dollar forty. But whereas our first well-known doctor's face was plump and round, his was plump and long: this was one great difference between them. Their use of medicine was different too. Our first well-known doctor's prescriptions could be prepared by one person, but no single person could cope satisfactorily with Dr. Chen's because his prescriptions always included a special pill or powder or an extra-special adjuvant.

Not once did be use reed roots or sugar-cane that had seen three years of frost. Most often it was "a pair of crickets," with a note in small characters at the side: "They must be an original pair, from the same burrow." So it seems that even insects must be chaste; if they marry again after losing their mates they forfeit even the right to be used as medicine. This task, however, presented no difficulties to me. In Hundred-Plant Garden I could catch ten pairs easily. I tied them with a thread and dropped them alive into the boiling pan, and that was that. But then there was "ten ardisia berries." Nobody knew what these were. I asked the pharmacy, I asked some peasants, I asked the vendor of herb medicines, I asked old people, I asked scholars, I asked a carpenter: but they all simply shook their

房的叔祖，爱种一点花木的老人，跑去一问，他果然知道，是生在山中树下的一种小树，能结红子如小珊瑚珠的，普通都称为“老弗大”。

“踏破铁鞋无觅处，得来全不费工夫。”药引寻到了，然而还有一种特别的丸药：败鼓皮丸。这“败鼓皮丸”就是用打破的旧鼓皮做成；水肿一名鼓胀，一用打破的鼓皮自然就可以克伏他。清朝的刚毅因为憎恨“洋鬼子”，预备打他们，练了些兵称作“虎神营”，取虎能食羊，神能伏鬼的意思，也就是这道理。可惜这一种神药，全城中只有一家出售的，离我家就有五里，但这却不像平地木那样，必须暗中摸索了，陈莲河先生开方之后，就恳切详细地给我们说明。

“我有一种丹，”有一回陈莲河先生说，“点在舌上，我想一定可以见效。因为舌乃心之灵苗……。价钱也并不贵，

heads. Last of all I remembered that distant great-uncle of mine, the old fellow who liked to grow flowers and trees, and hurried over to ask him. Sure enough, he knew: the ardisia was a shrub which grew at the foot of trees deep in the mountain. It had small red berrieslike coral beads, and was usually known as Never-Grow-Up.

> You wear out iron shoes in hunting round,
> When all the time it's easy to be found!

Now we had the adjuvant, but there was still a special pill: broken-drum bolus. Broken-drum boluses were made from the leather of worn-out drums. Since one name for "dropsy" is "drum-tight," the leather from worn-out drums can naturally cure it. Gangyi of the Qing Dynasty, who hated "foreign devils," acted on the same principle when he prepared to fight them by training a corps of "tiger angels," for the tigers would be able to eat the sheep, and the angels could subdue the devils. Unfortunately there was only one shop in the whole town which sold this miraculous drug, and that was nearly two miles from our house. However, this was not like the case of the ardisia which we groped in the dark to find. After making out his prescription Dr. Chen Lianhe gave me earnest and detailed instructions as to where to obtain it.

"I have one medicine," Dr. Chen told my father once, "which applied to the tongue would do you good, I'm sure. For the tongue is the intelligent

只要两块钱一盒……。”

我父亲沉思了一会，摇摇头。

“我这样用药还会不大见效，”有一回陈莲河先生又说，“我想，可以请人看一看，可有什么冤愆……。医能医病，不能医命，对不对？自然，这也许是前世的事……。”

我的父亲沉思了一会，摇摇头。

凡国手，都能够起死回生的，我们走过医生的门前，常可以看见这样的扁额。现在是让步一点了，连医生自己也说道：“西医长于外科，中医长于内科。”但是S城那时不但没有西医，并且谁也还没有想到天下有所谓西医，因此无论什么，都只能由轩辕岐伯的嫡派门徒包办。轩辕时候是巫医不分的，所以直到现在，他的门徒就还见鬼，而且觉得“舌乃心之灵苗”。这就是中国人的“命”，

sprout of the heart.... It is not expensive either, only two dollars a box...."

My father thought for some time, then shook his head.

"This present treatment may not prove too effective," said Dr. Chen another day. "I think we might ask a diviner if there is not some avenging spirit behind this....A doctor can cure diseases but not fate, isn't that correct? Of course, this may be something that happened in a previous existence...."

My father thought for some time, then shook his head.

All the best doctors can bring the dead to life, as we know from the placards hanging outside their houses which we see when we walk past. But now a concession has been made, for physicians themselves admit: "Western doctors are best at surgery, while Chinese doctors are best at internal medicine." But there was no Western-trained doctor in S — at that time. Indeed it had never occurred to anyone that there was such a thing in the world as a Western doctor. Hence, whenever anyone fell ill, all we could do was ask the direct descendants of the Yellow Emperor and Qi Bo to cure him. In the days of the Yellow Emperor, wizards and doctors were one; thus right down to the present his disciples can still see ghosts and believe that "the tongue is the intelligent sprout of the heart." This is the

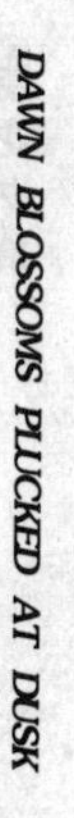

连名医也无从医治的。

不肯用灵丹点在舌头上，又想不出“冤愆”来，自然，单吃了一百多天的“败鼓皮丸”有什么用呢？依然打不破水肿，父亲终于躺在床上喘气了。还请一回陈莲河先生，这回是特拔，大洋十元。他仍旧泰然的开了一张方，但已停止败鼓皮丸不用，药引也不很神妙了，所以只消半天，药就煎好，灌下去，却从口角上回了出来。

从此我便不再和陈莲河先生周旋，只在街上有时看见他坐在三名轿夫的快轿里飞一般抬过；听说他现在还康健，一面行医，一面还做中医什么学报，正在和只长于外科的西医奋斗哩。

中西的思想确乎有一点不同。听说中国的孝子们，一到将要“罪孽深重祸延父母”的时候，就买几斤人参，煎汤灌下去，希望父母多喘几天气，即使半

"fate" of Chinese, which not even famous physicians are able to cure.

When he would not apply the efficacious remedy on his tongue and could not think of any avenging spirit he had wronged, naturally it was no use my father simply eating broken-drum boluses for over a hundred days. These drum pills proved unable to beat the dropsy, and finally my father lay at his last gasp on the bed. We invited Dr. Chen Lianhe once more — an emergency call this time, for ten silver dollars. Once more, he calmly wrote out a prescription. He discontinued the broken-drum boluses, however, and the adjuvant was too mysterious either; so before very long this medicine was ready. But when we poured it between my father's lips, it trickled out again from one side of his mouth.

That ended my dealings with Dr. Chen Lianhe; but I sometimes saw him in the street being carried swiftly by in his fast sedan-chair with three carriers. I hear he is still in good health, practising medicine and editing a paper on traditional Chinese medicine, engaging in a struggle with those Western-trained doctors who are good for nothing but surgery.

There is indeed a slight difference between the Chinese and Western outlook. I understand that when a filial son in China knows that his parents' end is approaching, he buys several catties of ginseng, boils it, and gives it to them, in the hope of

天也好。我的一位教医学的先生却教给我医生的职务道：可医的应该给他医治，不可医的应该给他死得没有痛苦。——但这先生自然是西医。

父亲的喘气颇长久，连我也听得很吃力，然而谁也不能帮助他。我有时竟至于电光一闪似的想道："还是快一点喘完了罢……。"立刻觉得这思想就不该，就是犯了罪；但同时又觉得这思想实在是正当的，我很爱我的父亲。便是现在，也还是这样想。

早晨，住在一门里的衍太太进来了。她是一个精通礼节的妇人，说我们不应该空等着。于是给他换衣服；又将纸锭和一种什么《高王经》烧成灰，用纸包了给他捏在拳头里……。

"叫呀，你父亲要断气了。快叫呀！"衍太太说。

"父亲！父亲！"我就叫起来。

"大声！他听不见。还不快叫?!"

"父亲！父亲!!"

他已经平静下去的脸，忽然紧张了，将眼微微一睁，仿佛有一些苦痛。

"叫呀！快叫呀！"她催促说。

prolonging their lives a few more days or even half a day. One of my professors, whose subject was medicine, told me that a doctor's duty was to cure those who could be cured, and see to it that those who could not die without suffering. But this professor, of course, was Western-trained.

Father's breathing became very laboured, until even I could scarcely bear to hear it; but nobody could help him. Sometimes the thought flashed into my mind, "Better if it could all be over quickly...." At once I knew I should not think of such a thing, in fact I felt guilty. But at the same time I felt this idea was only proper, for I loved my father dearly. Even today, I still feel the same about it.

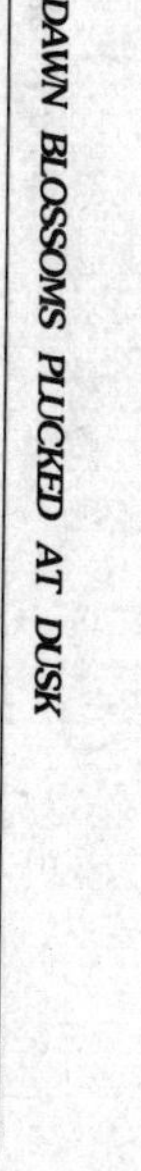

That morning Mrs. Yan, who lived in the same compound, came in. An authority on etiquette, she told us not to wait there doing nothing. So we changed his clothes, burnt paper coins and something called the *Gaowang Sutra*, and put the ashes, wrapped in paper, in his hand....

"Call him!" said Mrs. Yan. "Your father's at his last gasp. Call him quickly!"

"Father! Father!" I called accordingly.

"Louder, He can't hear. Hurry up, can't you?"

"Father! Father!"

His face, which had been composed, grew suddenly tense again; and he raised his eyelids slightly, as if in pain.

"Call him!" she insisted. "Hurry up and call

"父亲!!"

"什么呢?……不要嚷。……不……。"他低低地说,又较急地喘着气,好一会,这才复了原状,平静下去了。

"父亲!!"我还叫他,一直到他咽了气。

我现在还听到那时的自己的这声音,每听到时,就觉得这却是我对于父亲的最大的错处。

十月七日。

him!"

"Father!!!"

"What is it?... Don't shout....Don't...."

His voice was low, and once more he started panting for breath. It was some time before he recovered his earlier calm.

"Father!!!"

I went on calling until he breathed his last.

I can still hear my voice as it sounded then. And each time I hear those cries, I feel this was the greatest wrong I ever did my father.

October 7

琐 记

衍太太现在是早经做了祖母;也许竟做了曾祖母了,那时却还年青,只有一个儿子比我大三四岁。她对自己的儿子虽然狠,对别家的孩子却好的,无论闹出什么乱子来,也决不去告诉各人的父母,因此我们就最愿意在她家里或她家的四近玩。

举一个例说罢,冬天,水缸里结了薄冰的时候,我们大清早起一看见,便吃冰。有一回给沈四太太看到了,大声说道:“莫吃呀,要肚子疼的呢!”这声音又给我母亲听到了,跑出来我们都挨了一顿骂,并且有大半天不准玩。我们推论祸首,认定是沈四太太,于是提起她就不用尊称了,给她另外起了一个绰号,叫作“肚子疼”。

衍太太却决不如此。假如她看见我们吃冰,一定和蔼地笑着说,“好,再吃一块。我记着,看谁吃的多。”

Fragmentary Recollections

Mrs. Yan has long been a grandmother, and may even be a great-grandmother; but in those days she was still young, with just one son three or four years older than myself. Though very strict with her own son, she was kind to other people's children and no matter what trouble they made would never go to tell their parents. So we all liked to play in her house or in its vicinity.

To give one example. In winter, we noticed early one morning that a thin layer of ice had formed in the water vat, and we started eating the ice. Fourth Mrs. Shen, seeing us do this, cried: "Don't eat that! It'll give you bellyache." And my mother, hearing this, rushed out to give us all a scolding; moreover, we were forbidden to play there for hours. We decided that Fouth Mrs. Shen was the root of this trouble, so we stopped referring to her respectfully and gave her a new nickname "Bellyache."

Mrs. Yan, however, never behaved like that. If she saw us eating ice, she would say with a kindly smile: "All right, have another piece. I'll keep count to see who eats most."

但我对于她也有不满足的地方。一回是很早的时候了，我还很小，偶然走进她家去，她正在和她的男人看书。我走近去，她便将书塞在我的眼前道，“你看，你知道这是什么?”我看那书上画着房屋，有两个人光着身子仿佛在打架，但又不很像。正迟疑间，他们便大笑起来了。这使我很不高兴，似乎受了一个极大的侮辱，不到那里去大约有十多天。一回是我已经十多岁了，和几个孩子比赛打旋子，看谁旋得多。她就从旁计着数，说道，“好，八十二个了！再旋一个，八十三！好，八十四！……”但正在旋着的阿祥，忽然跌倒了，阿祥的婶母也恰恰走进来。她便接着说道，“你看，不是跌了么？不听我的话。我叫你不要旋，不要旋……。”

虽然如此，孩子们总还喜欢到她那里去。假如头上碰得肿了一大块的时候，去寻母亲去罢，好的是骂一通，再给擦一点药；坏的是没有药擦，还添几个栗凿和一通骂。衍太太却决不埋怨，立

Yet certain things about her displeased me too. One happened very early when I was still very small. Ihad chanced to go into her house when she and her husband were reading a book together. When I went up to her. She thrust the book under my nose and said: "Look. What do you think this is?" I saw in the book a picture of a house in which two naked people seemed to be fighting, and yet it didn't look exactly like fighting. As I was puzzling over this, they started roaring with laughter. This annoyed me immensely, for I felt greatly insulted, and for about ten days or more I did not go back there.

Another thing happened when I was over ten, competing with some other children to see which of us could spin round the most times. From the side she kept count: "Fine, eighty-two! Another spin, eighty-three! Fine, eighty-four!...." But Ah Xiang, the one spinning, suddenly fell down — just as his aunt happened to come into the room. At once Mrs. Yan said: "See, didn't I say you'd fall? You wouldn't listen to me. I told you not to do it, not to spin...."

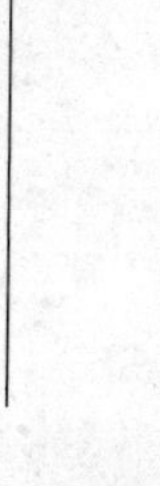

Nevertheless, children still liked to go to her place. If we knocked our heads and raised big bruises, then went to mother, she would at best give us a scolding, then rub on some ointment; but if she had no ointment we would get the scolding plus a few extra slaps. Mrs. Yan, however, never

刻给你用烧酒调了水粉，搽在疙瘩上，说这不但止痛，将来还没有瘢痕。

父亲故去之后，我也还常到她家里去，不过已不是和孩子们玩耍了，却是和衍太太或她的男人谈闲天。我其时觉得很有许多东西要买，看的和吃的，只是没有钱。有一天谈到这里，她便说道，“母亲的钱，你拿来用就是了，还不就是你的么？”我说母亲没有钱，她就说可以拿首饰去变卖；我说没有首饰，她却道，“也许你没有留心。到大厨的抽屉里，角角落落去寻去，总可以寻出一点珠子这类东西……。”

这些话我听去似乎很异样，便又不到她那里去了，但有时又真想去打开大厨，细细地寻一寻。大约此后不到一月，就听到一种流言，说我已经偷了家里的东西去变卖了，这实在使我觉得有如掉在冷水里。流言的来源，我是明白的，倘是现在，只要有地方发表，我总要骂出流言家的狐狸尾巴来，但那时太年

blamed us. She would promptly mix some powder with alcohol and apply this to the sore place, assuring us that this would not only stop the pain but prevent there being any scarin future.

After my father's death I went on going frequently to her house, only not to play with other children but to chat with her and her husband. At that time there were many things I would have liked to buy, things to read or eat, only I had no money. Once when I mentioned this, she said: "Just take some from your mother. Isn't her money yours?" When I told her my mother had no money, she said I could take her trinkets to raise money on them. When I told her there were no trinkets, she said: "Perhaps you haven't looked carefully. If you search the drawers of that big chest and odd corners of the room, you're bound to find a few pearls or things of that sort...."

This advice seemed to me so odd that once more I stopped going there. Sometimes, however, I was really tempted to open the big chest and make a thorough search. Probably it was less than a month after this that I heard a rumour to the effect that I'd been stealing things from home to raise money on. This really made me feel as if plunged into icy cold water. I knew the source of the rumour. Should such a thing happen now, provided I could find somewhere to publish by exposure, I would certainly unmask the rumourmonger. But at that time I

青，一遇流言，便连自己也仿佛觉得真是犯了罪，怕遇见人们的眼睛，怕受到母亲的爱抚。

好。那么，走罢！

但是，那里去呢？S城人的脸早经看熟，如此而已，连心肝也似乎有些了然。总得寻别一类人们去，去寻为S城人所诟病的人们，无论其为畜生或魔鬼。那时为全城所笑骂的是一个开得不久的学校，叫作中西学堂，汉文之外，又教些洋文和算学。然而已经成为众矢之的了；熟读圣贤书的秀才们，还集了《四书》的句子，做一篇八股来嘲诮它，这名文便即传遍了全城，人人当作有趣的话柄。我只记得那"起讲"的开头是：——

"徐子以告夷子曰：吾闻用夏变夷者，未闻变于夷者也。今也不然：鴂舌之音，闻其声，皆雅言也。……"

以后可忘却了，大概也和现今的国粹保存大家的议论差不多。但我对于这中

was too young. When slandered, I seemed to feel myself truly guilty of some crime, afraid to meet people's eyes, afraid to receive consolation from my mother.

All right, Then leave the place!

But where could I go? I knew all the people of S — by sight, and they didn't amount to much — I seemed to have seen through them. I must find people of a different type, a type detested by the people of S —, whether they were beasts or devils. At that time the whole town was scoffing at a newly opened school called the Chinese Western School where, in addition to Chinese, they taught foreign languages and mathematics. But already it had become a target for all. Some literati well-versed in the works of the sages even concocted *a bagu* essay by stringing together phrases from the Four Books'to deride it. This famous essay at once spread throughout the town, a fine topic of conversation for everyone. All I remember now is the start of the opening:

"Master Xu said to Mater Yi: I have heard of Chinese culture being used to change the barbarians, but not of us being changed by the barbarians. Now times have changed: uncouth bird-like tongues are all considered as polite languages...."

What followed I forget. Doubtless similar arguments to those of the present-day champions of our national essence. However, I too was dissatisfied with that Chinese-Western School, for it taught only

西学堂，却也不满足，因为那里面只教汉文、算学、英文和法文。功课较为别致的，还有杭州的求是书院，然而学费贵。

无须学费的学校在南京，自然只好往南京去。第一个进去的学校，目下不知道称为什么了，光复以后，似乎有一时称为雷电学堂，很像《封神榜》上"太极阵"、"混元阵"一类的名目。总之，一进仪凤门，便可以看见它那二十丈高的桅杆和不知多高的烟通。功课也简单，一星期中，几乎四整天是英文："It is a cat.""Is it a rat?"一整天是读汉文："君子曰，颍考叔可谓纯孝也已矣，爱其母，施及庄公。"一整天是做汉文：《知己知彼百战百胜论》，《颍考叔论》，《云从龙风从虎论》，《咬得菜根则百事可做论》。

初进去当然只能做三班生，卧室里是一桌一凳一床，床板只有两块。头二

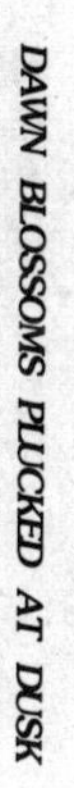

Chinese, mathematics, English and French. More uncommon subjects were taught in the Qiushi College in Hangzhou, but its fees were high.

The schools that asked for no fees were in Nanjing, so naturally I had to go to Nanjing. I do not know the present name of the school I first attended. I believe for a while, after the revolution, it was called the Thunder-and-Lightning School, a name reminiscent of such titles as "Primordial Ultimate Formation" or "Formless Void Formation" in the *Canonization of the Gods*. Anyway, as soon as one entered Yifeng Gate one could see its flagpole, two hundred feet high, and a chimney-shaft the height of which I do not know. The lessons were simple: virtually four whole days a week were spent on English: "It is a cat." "Is it a rat?" One whole day was spent on classical Chinese: "The Superior Man comments: Ying Kaoshu should be called a man of supreme piety, for loving his mother he extended that love to the prince." One whole day was spent on writing Chinese essays: "One Who Knows His Own Strength and That of the Enemy Is Invincible in Battle," "On Ying Kaoshu," "On How Clouds Follow the Dragon and Wind the Tiger," "One Content with Chewing Cabbage Root Can Accomplish All Things Under Heaven."

When I first entered school I was naturally put in the third or lowest grade. In my cubicle were one table, one stool and one bed, this latter consisting

班学生就不同了，二桌二凳或三凳一床，床板多至三块。不但上讲堂时挟着一堆厚而且大的洋书，气昂昂地走着，决非只有一本"泼赖妈"和四本《左传》的三班生所敢正视；便是空着手，也一定将肘弯撑开，像一只螃蟹，低一班的在后面总不能走出他之前。这一种螃蟹式的名公巨卿，现在都阔别得很久了，前四五年，竟在教育部的破脚躺椅上，发见了这姿势，然而这位老爷却并非雷电学堂出身的，可见螃蟹态度，在中国也颇普遍。

可爱的是桅杆。但并非如"东邻"的"支那通"所说，因为它"挺然翘然"，又是什么的象征。乃是因为它高，乌鸦喜鹊，都只能停在它的半途的木盘上。人如果爬到顶，便可以近看狮子山，远眺莫愁湖，——但究竟是否真可以眺得那么远，我现在可委实有点记不清楚了。而且不危险，下面张着网，即使跌下来，也不过如一条小鱼落在网子里；

of only two planks of wood. Students of the first and second grades were different, having two tables, two or three stools and one bed with as many as three planks. Not only did they stride with a lordly air to their classrooms, a pile of big, thick foreign books under their arms, quite unlike the third-grade students who took only one English primer and four volumes of *Zuo's Commentary to the "Spring and Autumn Annals"*; even when empty-handed they would walk with arms akimbo like crabs, making it impossible for a student of a lower grade to get past. It is some time now since I last met such crab-like swells. Four or five years ago I chanced to find an old gentleman in this posture on a broken-down chaise longue in the Ministry of Education, and the fact that he was not a graduate of the Thunder-and-Lightning School shows that this crab-like attitude is quite prevalent in China.

The flagpole was fine. Not because it was "standing erect," a symbol of something, as our "Eastern Neighbour's" sinologues would say. But because it was so tall that crows and magpies could only perch on the wooden disk halfway up it. If one climbed to the top, one could see Lion Mountain nearby and Sans-Souci Lake in the distance — but whether one could really see so far, I can't actually remember clearly now. Also there was no danger, for there was a net underneath and if one fell it would only be like a small fish falling into a net.

况且自从张网以后，听说也还没有人曾经跌下来。

原先还有一个池，给学生学游泳的，这里面却淹死了两个年幼的学生。当我进去时，早填平了，不但填平，上面还造了一所小小的关帝庙。庙旁是一座焚化字纸的砖炉，炉门上方横写着四个大字道："敬惜字纸"。只可惜那两个淹死鬼失了池子，难讨替代，总在左近徘徊，虽然已有"伏魔大帝关圣帝君"镇压着。办学的人大概是好心肠的，所以每年七月十五，总请一群和尚到雨天操场来放焰口，一个红鼻而胖的大和尚戴上毗卢帽，捏诀，念咒："回资罗，普弥耶吽！唵耶吽！唵！耶！吽！！！"

我的前辈同学被关圣帝君镇压了一整年，就只在这时候得到一点好处，——虽然我并不深知是怎样的好处。所以当这些时，我每每想：做学生总得自己小心些。

Besides, since the net had been set up there, I heard that no one had fallen.

There had orginally also been a pool where students could learn to swim. But two young students weredrowned there. By the time I went to the school the pool had been filled up, not only filled up, a small shrine to Lord Guan Yu had been built on the spot. Beside this shrine was a brick incinerator to burn waste paper with writing on it, and over its opening was the large horizontal inscription: "Respect Written Paper." It was unfortunate though that the filling up of the pool had denied the ghosts of the two drowned students the chance to find substitutes but forced them to haunt the place, even though there was "Sagacious and Imperial Lord Guan Yu the Conqueror of Devils" to control them. People who run schools are usually kindhearted, so each year on the fifteenth of the seventh month they always engaged a troop of monks to chant masses in the gymnasium. The corpulent, red-nosed chief monk, wearing his Buddhist headdress, would chant incantations: "*Hui-zi-le*, *pu-mi-ye-hum*! *Om-ye-hum*! *Om*! *Ye*! *Hum*!!!"

This was the only advantage enjoyed by those classmate predecessors of ours after being suppressed for a whole year by Lord Guan Yu — though I was not clear just where the advantage lay. So each time this happened I used to reflect that we students had better be more careful.

总觉得不大合适，可是无法形容出这不合适来。现在是发见了大致相近的字眼了，“乌烟瘴气”，庶几乎其可也。只得走开。近来是单是走开也就不容易，“正人君子”者流会说你骂人骂到了聘书，或者是发“名士”脾气，给你几句正经的俏皮话。不过那时还不打紧，学生所得的津贴，第一年不过二两银子，最初三个月的试习期内是零用五百文。于是毫无问题，去考矿路学堂去了，也许是矿路学堂，已经有些记不真，文凭又不在手头，更无从查考。试验并不难，录取的。

这回不是 It is a cat 了，是 Der Mann, Die Weib, Das Kind。汉文仍旧是“颍考叔可谓纯孝也已矣”，但外加《小学集注》。论文题目也小有不同，譬如《工欲善其事必先利其器论》是先前没有做过的。

此外还有所谓格致、地学、金石学、

It always seemed to me that something was not quite right, but I had no means of putting this into words. Now I have discovered a fairly close approximation: it seemed to me that it was "murky." So I had toleave. Nowadays it is not so easy just to leave. For "just minds and gentlemen" and the like will accuse you of getting a new contract form a college by cursing people or of posing as an "eccentric scholar," and they will pass high-minded, cutting remarks. At that time, though, it mattered less. A student's subsidy for the first year was only two taels of silver, and one got five hundred cash for expenses during the first three months on probation. So there was no problem, and I went to sit for the entrance examination of the School of Mining and Railways. At least, I think that was its name, but I cannot remember clearly, and no longer having my diploma with me I have no means of checking. The entrance test was not hard. I was accepted.

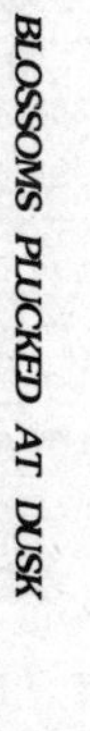

This time instead of "It is a cat," we learned "*Der Mann*, *Die Weib*, *Das Kind*." For Chinese, in addition to "Ying Kaoshu should be called a man of supreme piety," we also studied the *Etymological Lexicon with Commentaries*. Our essay subjects were slightly different too; for instance, "On the Need to Have Effective Tools to Do Good Work" was a subject we had never written on before.

Then there was physics, the science of the

……都非常新鲜。但是还得声明:后两项,就是现在之所谓地质学和矿物学,并非讲舆地和钟鼎碑版的。只是画铁轨横断面图却有些麻烦,平行线尤其讨厌。但第二年的总办是一个新党,他坐在马车上的时候大抵看着《时务报》,考汉文也自己出题目,和教员出的很不同。有一次是《华盛顿论》,汉文教员反而惴惴地来问我们道:“华盛顿是什么东西呀?……”

看新书的风气便流行起来,我也知道了中国有一部书叫《天演论》。星期日跑到城南去买下来,白纸石印的一厚本,价五百文正。翻开一看,是写得很好的字,开首便道:——

“赫胥黎独处一室之中,在英伦之南,背山而面野,槛外诸境,历历如在机下。乃悬想二千年前,当罗马大将恺彻未到时,此间有何景物?计惟有天造草昧……”

earth, the science of metals and stones... all these were quite novel. I must point out, however, that the last two were what we now call geology and mineralogy, not ancient geography or the study of bronze and stone inscriptions. Only drawing diagrams of cross-sections ofrails was rather troublesome, while parallel lines were even more tiresome. The director in the second year, however, was a Reformist Riding in his carriage he would usually read the *Contemporary Gazette*, and the subjects he set for Chinese examinations were quite different from those set by the teacher. Once he chose "On Washington." The disconcerted Chinese teacher had to come and ask us: "What is this thing, Washington?..."

Then it became fashionable to read new books, and I learned that there was a book called *Evolution and Ethics*. On Sunday I went to the south city and bought it: a thick volume lithographed on fine white paper, costing five hundred cash. Opening it — it was written in fine calligraphy — I read the preface:

"Huxley, alone in his room in southern England, with mountains behind the house and plains in front, had a fine view from his window. He wondered: What was this place like two thousand years ago, before Julius Caesar came here? There must have been nothing here but primitive waste-

哦！原来世界上竟还有一个赫胥黎坐在书房里那么想，而且想得那么新鲜？一口气读下去，“物竞”“天择”也出来了，苏格拉第、柏拉图也出来了，斯多噶也出来了。学堂里又设立了一个阅报处，《时务报》不待言，还有《译学汇编》，那书面上的张廉卿一流的四个字，就蓝得很可爱。

“你这孩子有点不对了，拿这篇文章去看去，抄下来去看去。”一位本家的老辈严肃地对我说，而且递过一张报纸来。接来看时，“臣许应骙跪奏……，”那文章现在是一句也不记得了，总之是参康有为变法的；也不记得可曾抄了没有。

仍然自己不觉得有什么“不对”，一有闲空，就照例地吃侉饼、花生米、辣椒，看《天演论》。

但我们也曾经有过一个很不平安的时期。那是第二年，听说学校就要裁撤了。这也无怪，这学堂的设立，原是

land. . . . ”

Well! So the world contained a man called Huxley who sat thinking in this way in his study and came up with such novel ideas! I read the book through at one sitting, and in it I found the “survival of the fittest,” and Socrates, Plato and the Stoics as well. The school had a reading-room where of course you could find the *Contemporary Gazette*; moreover, there was the magazine *Selected Translations*, its title written in the style of Zhang Lianqing’s school of calligraphy in a most attractive blue.

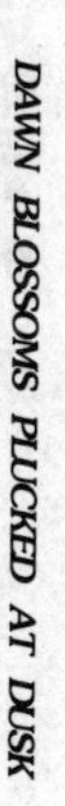

“Something is wrong with you, child. Take this article and read it, then copy it out,” one of my family elders ordered me sternly, passing me a newspaper. Taking it I read, “Your subject Xu Yingkui begs to report. . . .” I can’t remember a single sentence of that article now, but at all events it attacked Kang Youwei’s reforms. I can’t remember either whether I copied the article out or not.

I still did not feel that anything was “wrong” with me. Whenever I had time, I would as usual eat cakes, peanuts and paprika and read *Evolution and Ethics*.

But we also had one very unsettled period. That was during the second year, when we heard that the school was going to be closed. This was not strange, for this school had been set up because

因为两江总督(大约是刘坤一罢)听到青龙山的煤矿出息好,所以开手的。待到开学时,煤矿那面却已将原先的技师辞退,换了一个不甚了然的人了。理由是:一、先前的技师薪水太贵;二、他们觉得开煤矿并不难。于是不到一年,就连煤在那里也不甚了然起来,终于是所得的煤,只能供烧那两架抽水机之用,就是抽了水掘煤,掘出煤来抽水,结一笔出入两清的账。既然开矿无利,矿路学堂自然也就无须乎开了,但是不知怎的,却又并不裁撤。到第三年我们下矿洞去看的时候,情形实在颇凄凉,抽水机当然还在转动,矿洞里积水却有半尺深,上面也点滴而下,几个矿工便在这里面鬼一般工作着。

毕业,自然大家都盼望的,但一到毕业,却又有些爽然若失。爬了几次桅,不消说不配做半个水兵;听了几年讲,下了几回矿洞,就能掘出金、银、铜、铁、锡来么?实在连自己也茫无把握,

the Governor of Jiangnan and Jiangxi (probably Liu Kunyi) had heard that the Qinglongshan coal mine had good prospects. By the time the school opened, the mine had already dismissed its engineer and replaced him with someone not so adequate. Their reasons were: first, the original engineer's salary was too high; secondly, they felt it was easy to run a coal mine. So in less than a year, the output of coal became not so adequate too, until finally it was only enough to fuel the mine's two pumps; so water was pumped to get coal, and this coal wasused to pump water — the production and consumption were well balanced. Still, as the mine made no profit, there was naturally no need for a mining school. And yet, for some reason, the school was not closed. When we went down in our third year to see the pits, the sight was rather pathetic. Of course the pumps were still working, but water lay half a foot deep in the pit, more was dripping down from above, and the few miners toiling there looked like ghosts.

Of course we all looked forward to graduation. But when the time came, we felt rather let down. We had climbed the flagpole several times, but needless to say were not half qualified to be sailors; we had attended lectures for several years and been down the pits several times, but could we mine gold, silver, copper, iron or lead? The fact was,

没有做《工欲善其事必先利其器论》的那么容易。爬上天空二十丈和钻下地面二十丈，结果还是一无所能，学问是“上穷碧落下黄泉，两处茫茫皆不见”了。所余的还只有一条路：到外国去。

留学的事，官僚也许可了，派定五名到日本去。其中的一个因为祖母哭得死去活来，不去了，只剩了四个。日本是同中国很两样的，我们应该如何准备呢？有一个前辈同学在，比我们早一年毕业，曾经游历过日本，应该知道些情形。跑去请教之后，他郑重地说：——

“日本的袜是万不能穿的，要多带些中国袜。我看纸票也不好，你们带去的钱不如都换了他们的现银。”

四个人都说遵命。别人不知其详，我是将钱都在上海换了日本的银元，还带了十双中国袜——白袜。

后来呢？后来，要穿制服和皮鞋，

we had no such faith ourselves, for this was not as simple as writing an essay "On the Need to Have Effective Tools to Do Good Work." We had climbed two hundred feet into the sky and burrowed two hundred feet into the earth, but the result was that we still could do nothing. Knowledge was something that "could not be found even by searching the blue sky above and the yellow springs below." Only one course was left to us: to go abroad.

The authorities approved of study abroad, and agreed to send five students to Japan. But one of these five did not go, because his grandmother wept as if it would kill her. That left just four of us. Japan was verydifferent from China; how should we prepare ourselves? A student who had graduated a year ahead of us had been to Japan; he should know something of conditions there. When we went to ask his advice he told us earnestly:

"Japanese socks are absolutely unwearable, so take plenty of Chinese socks. And I don't think bank-notes are any good; better change all the money you take into their silver yen."

The four of us all agreed. I don't know about the others, but I changed all my money in Shanghai into Japanese silver yen, and I took with me ten pairs of Chinese socks, white cloth socks.

And later? Later we had to wear uniforms and leather shoes, so those cloth Chinese socks proved

中国袜完全无用;一元的银圆日本早已废置不用了,又赔钱换了半元的银圆和纸票。

十月八日。

completely useless. And as they had long given up using silver coins of the one-yuan denomination in Japan, I changed mine at a loss into half-yuan coins and bank-notes.

October 8

藤野先生

东京也无非是这样。上野的樱花烂熳的时节，望去确也像绯红的轻云，但花下也缺不了成群结队的“清国留学生”的速成班，头顶上盘着大辫子，顶得学生制帽的顶上高高耸起，形成一座富士山。也有解散辫子，盘得平的，除下帽来，油光可鉴，宛如小姑娘的发髻一般，还要将脖子扭几扭。实在标致极了。

中国留学生会馆的门房里有几本书买，有时还值得去一转；倘在上午，里面的几间洋房里倒也还可以坐坐的。但到傍晚，有一间的地板便常不免要咚咚咚地响得震天，兼以满房烟尘斗乱；问问精通时事的人，答道，“那是在学跳舞。”

到别的地方去看看，如何呢？

我就往仙台的医学专门学校去。

Mr. Fujino

Tokyo was not so extraordinary after all. When cherryblossom shimmered in Ueno, from the distance it actually resembled light, pink clouds; but under the flowers you would always find groups of short-term "students from the Qing Empire," their long queues coiled on top of their heads upraising the crowns of their student caps to look like Mount Fuji. Others had undone their queues and arranged their hair flat on their heads, so that when their caps were removed it glistened for all the world like the lustrous locks of young ladies; and they would toss their heads too. It was really a charming sight.

In the gatehouse of the Chinese students' hostel there were always some books on sale, and it was worth going there sometimes. In the mornings you could sit and rest in the foreign-style rooms inside. But towards the evening the floor of one room would often be shaken by a deafening tramp of feet, and dust would fill the whole place. If you questioned those in the know, the answer would be: "They are learning ballroom dancing."

Then why not go somewhere else?

So I went to the Medical College in Sendai.

从东京出发，不久便到一处驿站，写道：日暮里。不知怎地，我到现在还记得这名目。其次却只记得水户了，这是明的遗民朱舜水先生客死的地方。仙台是一个市镇，并不大；冬天冷得利害；还没有中国的学生。

大概是物以稀为贵罢。北京的白菜运往浙江，便用红头绳系住菜根，倒挂在水果店头，尊为“胶菜”；福建野生着的芦荟，一到北京就请进温室，且美其名曰“龙舌兰”。我到仙台也颇受了这样的优待，不但学校不收学费，几个职员还为我的食宿操心。我先是住在监狱旁边一个客店里的，初冬已经颇冷，蚊子却还多，后来用被盖了全身，用衣服包了头脸，只留两个鼻孔出气。在这呼吸不息的地方，蚊子竟无从插嘴，居然睡安稳了。饭食也不坏。但一位先生却以为这客店也包办囚人的饭食，我住在那里不相宜，几次三番，几次三

Soon after leaving Tokyo I came to a station called Nippori; somehow or other, even now I remember the name. The next place I remember was Mito, where Zhu Shunshui who was loyal to the Ming Dynasty after its downfall died in exile. Sendai was a small market town, very cold in the winter, with as yet no Chinese students studying there.

No doubt the rarer a thing the higher its value. When Peking cabbage is shipped to Zhejiang, it is hung upside-down in the greengrocer's by a red string tied to its root, and given the grand title "Shandong Vegetable." When the aloe which grows wild in Fujian comes to Peking, it is ushered into a hothouse and given the beautiful name "Dragon-Tongue Orchid." In Sendai I too enjoyed such preferential treatment; not only did the school not ask for fees, but several members of the staff even showed great concern over my board and lodging. At first I stayed in an inn next to the gaol, where although the early winter was already quite cold, there were still a good many mosquitoes, so I learned to cover myself completely with the quilt and wrap my clothes round my head, leaving only two nostrils exposed through which to breathe. In this area, shaken by my continuous breathing, mosquitoes could find no place to bite; thus I slept soundly. The food was not bad either. But one of our staff thought that since this inn also catered for the convicts, it was not fitting for me to stay there; and he pleaded with me earnestly

番地说。我虽然觉得客店兼办囚人的饭食和我不相干，然而好意难却，也只得别寻相宜的住处了。于是搬到别一家，离监狱也很远，可惜每天总要喝难以下咽的芋梗汤。

从此就看见许多陌生的先生，听到许多新鲜的讲义。解剖学是两个教授分任的。最初是骨学。其时进来的是一个黑瘦的先生，八字须，戴着眼镜，挟着一迭大大小小的书。一将书放在讲台上，便用了缓慢而很有顿挫的声调，向学生介绍自己道：——

"我就是叫作藤野严九郎的……。"

后面有几个人笑起来了。他接着便讲述解剖学在日本发达的历史，那些大大小小的书，便是从最初到现今关于这一门学问的著作。起初有几本是线装的；还有翻刻中国译本的，他们的翻译和研究新的医学，并不比中国早。

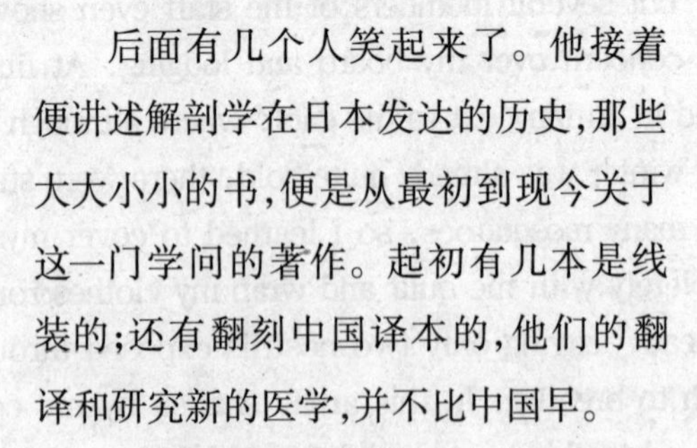

那坐在后面发笑的是上学年不及格的留级学生，在校已经一年，掌故颇为熟悉的了。他们便给新生讲演每个

time and again. Though I considered the fact that this inn also catered for the convicts had nothing to do with me, I could not ignore his kindness, so I had to look for a more fitting place. Thus I moved to another house a long way from the gaol, where unfortunately I had to drink taro tuber soup every day, which I found rather hard to swallow.

After this I met many new teachers and attended many new lectures. The anatomy course was taught by two professors. First came osteology. There entered a dark, lean instructor with a moustache, who was wearing glasses and carrying under his arm a pile of books, large and small. Having set the books on the table, in slow and most measured tones he introduced himself to the class:

"My name is Fujino Genkuro...."

Some students at the back started laughing. He went on to outline the history of the development of anatomical science in Japan, those books, large and small, being works published on this subject form the earliest time till then. There were first a few books in old-fashioned binding, then some Chinese translations reprinted in Japan. So they had not started translating and studying new medical science any earlier than in China.

Those sitting at the back and laughing were students who had failed the previous term and been kept down, who after one year in the college knew a great many stories. They proceeded to ragale the

教授的历史。这藤野先生，据说是穿衣服太模胡了，有时竟会忘记带领结；冬天是一件旧外套，寒颤颤的，有一回上火车去，致使管车的疑心他是扒手，叫车里的客人大家小心些。

他们的话大概是真的，我就亲见他有一次上讲堂没有带领结。

过了一星期，大约是星期六，他使助手来叫我了。到得研究室，见他坐在人骨和许多单独的头骨中间，——他其时正在研究着头骨，后来有一篇论文在本校的杂志上发表出来。

“我的讲义，你能抄下来么？”他问。

“可以抄一点。”

“拿来我看！”

我交出所抄的讲义去，他收下了，第二三天便还我，并且说，此后每一星期要送给他看一回。我拿下来打开看时，很吃了一惊，同时也感到一种不安和感激。原来我的讲义已经从头到末，都用红笔添改过了，不但增加了许多脱漏的地方，连文法的错误，也都一一订

freshmen with the history of every professor. This Mr. Fujino, they said, dressed so carelessly that he sometimes even forgot to put on a tie. Because he shivered all winter in an old overcoat, once when he travelled by train the conductor suspected him of being a pickpocket and warned all the passengers to be on their guard.

What they said was probably true: I myself saw him come to class once without a tie.

A week later, on a Saturday I think, he sent his assistant for me. I found him sitting in his laboratory among skeletons and a number of separate skulls — he was studying skulls at the time and later published a monograph on the subject in the college journal.

"Can you take notes of my lectures?" he asked.

"After a fashion."

"Let me see them."

I gave him the notes I had taken, and he kept them, to return them a day or two later with the instruction that henceforth I should hand them in every week. When I took them back and looked at them, I received a great surprise, and felt at the same time both embarrassed and grateful. From beginning to end my notes had been supplemented and corrected in red ink. Not only had he added a great deal I had missed, he had even corrected every single grammatical mistake. And so it went on till he

正。这样一直继续到教完了他所担任的功课:骨学、血管学、神经学。

可惜我那时太不用功,有时也很任性。还记得有一回藤野先生将我叫到他的研究室里去,翻出我那讲义上的一个图来,是下臂的血管,指着,向我和蔼的说道:——

"你看,你将这条血管移了一点位置了。——自然,这样一移,的确比较的好看些,然而解剖图不是美术,实物是那么样的,我们没法改换它。现在我给你改好了,以后你要全照着黑板上那样的画。"

但是我还不服气,口头答应着,心里却想道:——

"图还是我画的不错;至于实在的情形,我心里自然记得的。"

学年试验完毕之后,我便到东京玩了一夏天,秋初再回学校,成绩早已发表了,同学一百余人之中,我在中间,不过是没有落第。这回藤野先生所担任的功课,是解剖实习和局部解剖学。

解剖实习了大概一星期,他又叫我去了,很高兴地,仍用了极有抑扬的声调对我说道:——

"我因为听说中国人是很敬重鬼

had taught all the courses for which he was responsible: osteology, angiology, neurology.

Unfortunately, I was not in the least hardworking, and was sometimes most self-willed. I remember once Mr. Fujino called me to his laboratory and showed me a diagram in my notes of the blood vessels of the forearm. Pointing at this, he said kindly:

"Look, you have moved this blood vessel a little out of place. Of course, when moved like this it does look better; but anatomical charts are not works of art, and we have no way of altering real things. I have corrected it for you, and in future you should copy exactly from the blackboard."

I was very stubborn, however. Though I assented, I was thinking:

"My diagram was a good drawing. As for the true facts, of course I can remember them."

After the annual examination I spent the summer enjoying myself in Tokyo. By early autumn, when I went back to the college, the results had long since been published. I came halfway down the list of more than a hundred students, but I had not failed. This term Mr. Fujino's courses were practical anatomy and topographic anatomy.

After roughly a week of practical anatomy he sent for me again and, looking very gratified, said, still in the most measured tones:

"Having heard what respect the Chinese show

的,所以很担心,怕你不肯解剖尸体。现在总算放心了,没有这回事。”

但他也偶有使我很为难的时候。他听说中国的女人是裹脚的,但不知道详细,所以要问我怎么裹法,足骨变成怎样的畸形,还叹息道,“总要看一看才知道。究竟是怎么一回事呢?”

有一天,本级的学生会干事到我寓里来了,要借我的讲义看。我检出来交给他们,却只翻检了一遍,并没有带走。但他们一走,邮差就送到一封很厚的信,拆开看时,第一句是:——

“你改悔罢!”

这是《新约》上的句子罢,但经托尔斯泰新近引用过的。其时正值日俄战争,托老先生便写了一封给俄国和日本的皇帝的信,开首便是这一句。日本报纸上很斥责他的不逊,爱国青年也愤然,然而暗地里却早受了他的影响了。其次的话,大略是说上年解剖学试验的

to spirits, I was afraid you might be unwilling to dissect corpses. Now my mind is at rest, since this is not the case."

Yet sometimes too, inadvertently, he embarrassed me very much. He had heard that Chinese women had bound feet, but did not know the details; so he wanted to learn from me how it was done, how the bones in the feet were deformed. And he said with a sigh, "I should have to see it to understand. What can it really be like?"

One day the executives of the students' union of my class came to my hostel and asked to borrow my lecture notes. I found them and handed them over, but they merely looked through the notes without taking them away. As soon as they left, however, the postman delivered a bulky envelope, and when I opened it, the first line read:

"Repent!"

This was probably a quotation from the New Testament, but it had recently been used by Tolstoy. It was then the time of the Russo-Japanese War, and Count Tolstory wrote to both the Russian tsar and the Japanese mikado, opening his letter with this word. The Japanese papers denounced him roundly for his presumption; patriotic youths were most indignant too, though they had been influenced by him without knowing it. The rest of the letter was to the effect that the question for our anatomy test the previous year had been marked by

题目,是藤野先生讲义上做了记号,我预先知道的,所以能有这样的成绩。末尾是匿名。

我这才回忆到前几天的一件事。因为要开同级会,干事便在黑板上写广告,末一句是“请全数到会勿漏为要”,而且在“漏”字旁边加了一个圈。我当时虽然觉到圈得可笑,但是毫不介意,这回才悟出那字也在讥刺我了,犹言我得了教员漏泄出来的题目。

我便将这事告知了藤野先生;有几个和我熟识的同学也很不平,一同去诘责干事托辞检查的无礼,并且要求他们将检查的结果,发表出来。终于这流言消灭了,干事却又竭力运动,要收回那一封匿名信去。结末是我便将这托尔斯泰式的信退还了他们。

中国是弱国,所以中国人当然是低能儿,分数在六十分以上,便不是自己的能力了:也无怪他们疑惑。但我接着便有参观枪毙中国人的命运了。第二

Mr. Fujino on my lecture notes, and itwas because I knew them beforehand that I was able to pass. The letter was unsigned.

Then I recalled an incident a few days earlier. Because there was to be a meeting of our whole class, the students' executive had written an announcement on the blackboard, concluding with the words: "Please come without fail, and let there be no *leakage*." The word "leakage" was underlined. Though I thought at the time that this underlining was funny, I paid no attention to it; now I realized it was directed against me too. Implying that I had got hold of the questions through some leakage on the part of our teacher.

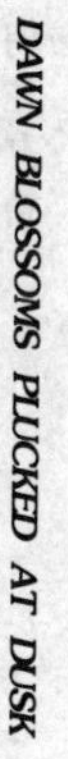

I reported this to Mr. Fujino. A few students who knew me well were indignant too, and we protested to the executives against their rudeness in examining my notes under another pretext, and demanded that they publish the results of their investigation. So finally the rumour died, the executives tried by every means to recover that anonymous letter, and in the end I returned them their Tolstoyan missive.

China is a weak country, therefore the Chinese must be an inferior people, and for a Chinese to get more than sixty marks could not be due simply to his own efforts. No wonder they suspected me. But soon after this it was my fate to watch the execution of some Chinese. In our second year we had a new

年添教霉菌学，细菌的形状是全用电影来显示的，一段落已完而还没有到下课的时候，便影几片时事的片子，自然都是日本战胜俄国的情形。但偏有中国人夹在里边：给俄国人做侦探，被日本军捕获，要枪毙了，围着看的也是一群中国人；在讲堂里的还有一个我。

“万岁！”他们都拍掌欢呼起来。

这种欢呼，是每看一片都有的，但在我，这一声却特别听得刺耳。此后回到中国来，我看见那些闲看枪毙犯人的人们，他们也何尝不酒醉似的喝采，——呜呼，无法可想！但在那时那地，我的意见却变化了。

到第二学年的终结，我便去寻藤野先生，告诉他我将不学医学，并且离开这仙台。他的脸色仿佛有些悲哀，似乎想说话，但竟没有说。

“我想去学生物学，先生教给我的学问，也还有用的。”其实我并没有决意要学生物学，因为看得他有些凄然，便说了一个慰安他的谎话。

course, bacteriology. All the bacterial forms were shown in slides, and if we completed one section before it was time for the class to be dismissed, some news in slides would be shown. Naturally at that time they were all about the Japanese victories over the Russians. But in these lantern slides there were also scenes of some Chinese who had acted as spies for Russians and were captured by the Japanese and shot, while other Chinese looked on. And there was I, too, in the classroom.

"*Banzai*!" The students clapped their hands and cheered.

They cheered everything we saw; but to me the cheering that day was unusually jarring to my ear. Later when I came back to China I saw idlers watching criminals being shot, who also cheered as if they were drunk. Alas, there is nothing one can do about it. At that time and in that place, however, it made me change my mind.

At the end of my second year I called on Mr. Fujino to tell him I was going to stop studying medicine and leave Sendai. A shadow crossed his face and he seemed on the point of speaking, but then thought better of it.

"I want to study biology, so what you have taught me, sir, will still be useful." As a matter of fact, I had no intention of studying biology; but seeing he looked rather sad I told this lie to comfort him.

"为医学而教的解剖学之类，怕于生物学也没有什么大帮助。"他叹息说。

将走的前几天，他叫我到他家里去，交给我一张照相，后面写着两个字道："惜别"，还说希望将我的也送他。但我这时适值没有照相了；他便叮嘱我将来照了寄给他，并且时时通信告诉他此后的状况。

我离开仙台之后，就多年没有照过相，又因为状况也无聊，说起来无非使他失望，便连信也怕敢写了。经过的年月一多，话更无从说起，所以虽然有时想写信，却又难以下笔，这样的一直到现在，竟没有寄过一封信和一张照片。从他那一面看起来，是一去之后，杳无消息了。

但不知怎地，我总还时时记起他，在我所认为我师的之中，他是最使我感激，给我鼓励的一个。有时我常常想：他的对于我的热心的希望，不倦的教诲，小而言之，是为中国，就是希望中国有新的医学；大而言之，是为学术，就是

"I fear subjects like the anatomy taught to medical students will not be of much help to you in the study of biology," he said with a sigh.

A few days before I left he called me to his house, gave me a photograph on the back of which he had written "Farewell," and said he hoped I would give him one of mine. Since I had no photographs at that time, he told me to send him one later when I had taken one, and to write to him regularly to tell him how I was doing.

After leaving Sendai I did not have a photograph taken for many years, and since there was nothing gratifying in my life and telling him would only disappoint him, I did not even dare write to him. As the months and years slipped by, there was so much to tell that I felt more perplexed for words; so though sometimes I wanted to write I found it hard to begin, and I have not yet written him a single letter nor sent him a photograph. As far as he is concerned, he must think I have disappeared for good.

But somehow or other I still remember him form time to time, for of all those whom I consider as my teachers he is the one to whom I feel most grateful and who gave me the most encouragement. And I often think: the keen faith he had in me and his indefatigable help were in a limited sense for China, for he wanted China to have modern medical science; but in larger sense they were for science,

希望新的医学传到中国去。他的性格，在我的眼里和心里是伟大的，虽然他的姓名并不为许多人所知道。

他所改正的讲义，我曾经订成三厚本，收藏着的，将作为永久的纪念。不幸七年前迁居的时候，中途毁坏了一口书箱，失去半箱书，恰巧这讲义也遗失在内了。责成运送局去找寻，寂无回信。只有他的照相至今还挂在我北京寓居的东墙上，书桌对面。每当夜间疲倦，正想偷懒时，仰面在灯光中瞥见他黑瘦的面貌，似乎正要说出抑扬顿挫的话来，便使我忽又良心发现，而且增加勇气了，于是点上一枝烟，再继续写些为"正人君子"之流所深恶痛疾的文字。

十月十二日。

for he wanted modern medical knowledge to spread to China. In my eyes he is a great man, and I feel this in my heart, though his name is not known to many people.

I had the lecture notes he corrected bound into three thick volumes and kept them as a permanent souvenir. Unfortunately seven years ago when I was moving house, a case of books broken open on the road and half the contents were lost including these notes. I asked the transport company to make a search, but to no effect. So all I have left is his photograph which hangs on the east wall of my Peking lodging, opposite my desk. At night if I am tired and want to take it easy, when I look up and see his thin, dark face in the lamplight, as if about to speak in measured tones, my better nature asserts itself and my courage returns. Then I light a cigarette, and write some more of those articles so hated and detested by "just minds and gentlemen."

October 12

范 爱 农

在东京的客店里，我们大抵一起来就看报。学生所看的多是《朝日新闻》和《读卖新闻》，专爱打听社会上琐事的就看《二六新闻》。一天早晨，辟头就看见一条从中国来的电报，大概是：——

“安徽巡抚恩铭被 Jo Shiki Rin 刺杀，刺客就擒。”

大家一怔之后，便容光焕发地互相告语，并且研究这刺客是谁，汉字是怎样三个字。但只要是绍兴人，又不专看教科书的，却早已明白了。这是徐锡麟，他留学回国之后，在做安徽候补道，办着巡警事务，正合于刺杀巡抚的地位。

大家接着就预测他将被极刑，家族

Fan Ainong

In our lodgings in Tokyo, we usually read the papers as soon as we got up. Most students read the *Asahi Shimbun* and the *Yomiuri Shimbum*, while those with a passion for tittle-tattle read the *Niroku Shimbun*. One morning, the first thing our eyes lit on was a telegram from China, much as follows:

"Enming, Governor of Anhui, has been assassinated by Jo Shiki Rin. The assassin has been captured."

After the initial shock, all the students brightened up and started chatting away. They also tried to work out who the assassin was, and what were the three Chinese characters translated as Jo Shiki Rin. But everyone from Shaoxing who read anything more than textbooks had understood at once. This was Xu Xilin who, after finishing his studies and returning to China, had been in charge of police administration as commissioner designate of Anhui — he was just in the position to assassinate the governor.

Everybody went on to prophesy that he would receive the extreme penalty, and his whole clan

将被连累。不久,秋瑾姑娘在绍兴被杀的消息也传来了,徐锡麟是被挖了心,给恩铭的亲兵炒食净尽。人心很愤怒。有几个人便秘密地开一个会,筹集川资;这时用得着日本浪人了,撕乌贼鱼下酒,慷慨一通之后,他便登程去接徐伯荪的家属去。

照例还有一个同乡会,吊烈士,骂满洲;此后便有人主张打电报到北京,痛斥满政府的无人道。会众即刻分成两派:一派要发电,一派不要发。我是主张发电的,但当我说出之后,即有一种钝滞的声音跟着起来:——

"杀的杀掉了,死的死掉了,还发什么屁电报呢。"

这是一个高大身材,长头发,眼球白多黑少的人,看人总像在渺视。他蹲在席子上,我发言大抵就反对;我早觉得奇怪,注意着他的了,到这时才打听别人:说这话的是谁呢,有那么冷?认识的人告诉我说:他叫范爱农,是徐伯

would be involved. Not long after this, news also reached us that Miss Qiu Jin had been executed in Shaoxing, and XuXilin's heart had been torn out, fried and eaten by Enming's bodyguards. We were furious. Some of us held a secret meeting to raise passage money, for this was where a Japanese ronin would come in useful. When he was in a jovial mood, after tearing up cuttlefish to go with his wine, he set out to fetch Xu's family.

As usual, we also held a meeting of fellow provincials to mourn for the revolutionary martyrs and abuse the Manzhu government. Then someone proposed sending a telegram to Peking to inveigh against the Manzhu government's inhumanity. At once the meeting divided into two camps: those in favour of sending a telegram, and those against it. I was in favour, but after I had expressed my opinion, a deep, gruff voice declared:

"Those killed have been killed, those dead have died — what's the use of sending a stinking telegram?"

The speaker was a tall, burly fellow with long hair and more white than black to his eyes, who always seemed to be looking at people contemptuously. Squatting on the mat, he opposed almost all I said. This had struck me before as strange, and I had my eyes on him, but only now did I ask:

"Who was that last speaker, who's so cold?"

Someone who knew him told me: "That's Fan

荪的学生。

我非常愤怒了，觉得他简直不是人，自己的先生被杀了，连打一个电报还害怕，于是便坚执地主张要发电，同他争起来。结果是主张发电的居多数，他屈服了。其次要推出人来拟电稿。

“何必推举呢？自然是主张发电的人罗～～。”他说。

我觉得他的话又在针对我，无理倒也并非无理的。但我便主张这一篇悲壮的文章必须深知烈士生平的人做，因为他比别人关系更密切，心里更悲愤，做出来就一定更动人。于是又争起来。结果是他不做，我也不做，不知谁承认做去了；其次是大家走散，只留下一个拟稿的和一两个干事，等候做好之后去拍发。

从此我总觉得这范爱农离奇，而且很可恶。天下可恶的人，当初以为是满人，这时才知道还在其次；第一倒是范

Ainong, one of Xu Xilin's students."

This was outrageous — the fellow was simply not human! His teacher had been murdered, yet he did not even dare send a telegram. Thereupon I absolutely insisted on sending one, and began to argue with him. The result was that those in favour of sending a telegram were in the majority, and he had to give way. The next thing was to vote for someone to draft it.

"Why bother to vote?" he asked. "Of course it should be the one who proposed sending a telegram."

I was sure this remark was also aimed at me, though it was not unreasonable. However, I declared it was essential that a composition of such a tragic nature be written by someone thoroughly familiar with the life of the martyr, for the fact that he had a closer relationship and felt more distressed and indignant than other people would certainly make his writing much more moving. So I began to argue with him again. The result was that neither he nor I drafted it. I forget who consented to draft it. The next thing was that everyone left except the man drawing up the telegram and one or two helpers who would send it off when it was written.

After that I always found this Fan Ainong unnatural, and most detestable. I had formerly thought the most detestable people in the world were the Manzhus, but now I realized they were

爱农。中国不革命则已，要革命，首先就必须将范爱农除去。

然而这意见后来似乎逐渐淡薄，到底忘却了，我们从此也没有再见面。直到革命的前一年，我在故乡做教员，大概是春末时候罢，忽然在熟人的客座上看见了一个人，互相熟视了不过两三秒钟，我们便同时说：——

"哦哦，你是范爱农！"

"哦哦，你是鲁迅！"

不知怎地我们便都笑了起来，是互相的嘲笑和悲哀。他眼睛还是那样，然而奇怪，只这几年，头上却有了白发了，但也许本来就有，我先前没有留心到。他穿着很旧的布马褂，破布鞋，显得很寒素。谈起自己的经历来，他说他后来没有了学费，不能再留学，便回来了。回到故乡之后，又受着轻蔑，排斥，迫害，几乎无地可容。现在是躲在乡下，

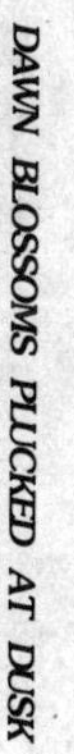

still secondary: the primary offender was Fan Ainong. If China had no revolution, no more need be said on the matter. If there was a revolution, the first thing to do was to root out Fan Ainong.

Later, however, my views on this subject seem by degrees to have weakened, to be finally forgotten, and after that we never met again. Not till the year before the revolution, when I was teaching in my hometown. There at the end of the spring, I think, I suddenly saw a man in a friend's house whose face looked very familiar. After staring at each other for not more than two or three seconds, we both exclaimed:

"Why, you're Fan Ainong!"

"Why, you're Lu Xun!"

I don't know why, but we both started laughing at that — laughing at ourselves and regretting the days that had gone. His eyes were still the same; but strangely enough, though only a few years had passed, he already had some white hairs. Or maybe his hair had been white all the time, only I had never noticed. Wearing a very old cloth jacket and worn-out cloth shoes, he looked extremely shabby. Speaking of his experiences, he told me he had run out of money later, so that he could not continue his studies but had to come home. After his return he had been depised, rejected and persecuted — virtually no place would have him. Now he was taking refuge in the country, making a meagre

教着几个小学生糊口。但因为有时觉得很气闷,所以也趁了航船进城来。

他又告诉我现在爱喝酒,于是我们便喝酒。从此他每一进城,必定来访我,非常相熟了。我们醉后常谈些愚不可及的疯话,连母亲偶然听到了也发笑。一天我忽而记起在东京开同乡会时的旧事,便问他:——

"那一天你专门反对我,而且故意似的,究竟是什么缘故呢?"

"你还不知道?我一向就讨厌你的,——不但我,我们。"

"你那时之前,早知道我是谁么?"

"怎么不知道。我们到横滨,来接的不就是子英和你么?你看不起我们,摇摇头,你自己还记得么?"

我略略一想,记得的,虽然是七八年前的事。那时是子英来约我的,说到横滨去接新来留学的同乡。汽船一到,看见一大堆,大概一共有十多人,一上岸便将行李放到税关上去候查检,关吏在衣箱中翻来翻去,忽然翻出一双绣花

living by teaching a few small boys. But he sometimes felt so depressed that he took a boat to town.

He told me also that he now liked drinking, so we drank. After that, whenever he came to town he would look me up, till we knew each other very well. In our cups we often said such crazy, senseless things that even my mother would laugh when she happened to hear us. One day I suddenly remembered that meeting of our fellow provincials in Tokyo.

"Why did you do nothing but oppose me that day, as if deliberately?" I asked him.

"Don't you know? I always disliked you — not just I, but all of us."

"Did you know who I was before that?"

"Of course. When we arrived at Yokohama, didn't you come with Chen Ziying to meet us? You shook your head over us contemptuously — don't you remember that?"

After a little thought I remembered, although it had happedned seven or eight years ago. Chen Ziying had called for me, saying we must go to Yokohama to meet some fellow provincials who were coming to study in Japan. As soon as the steamer arrived I saw a large group of probably more than a dozen of them. Once ashore, they took their baggage to the customhouse, and while looking through their cases the customs officer suddenly found a pair of embroidered slippers for a woman with bound

的弓鞋来，便放下公事，拿着仔细地看。我很不满，心里想，这些鸟男人，怎么带这东西来呢。自已不注意，那时也许就摇了摇头。检验完毕，在客店小坐之后，即须上火车。不料这一群读书人又在客车上让起座位来了，甲要乙坐在这位上，乙要丙去坐，揖让未终，火车已开，车身一摇，即刻跌倒了三四个。我那时也很不满，暗地里想：连火车上的座位，他们也要分出尊卑来……。自已不注意，也许又摇了摇头。然而那群雍容揖让的人物中就有范爱农，却直到这一天才想到。岂但他呢，说起来也惭愧，这一群里，还有后来在安徽战死的陈伯平烈士，被害的马宗汉烈士；被囚在黑狱里，到革命后才见天日而身上永带着匪刑的伤痕的也还有一两人。而我都茫无所知，摇着头将他们一并运上东京了。徐伯荪虽然和他们同船来，却不在这车上，因为他在神户就和他的夫人坐车走了陆路了。

feet, and set aside his public duties to pick these up and examine them curiously. I was very annoyed, and thought: "What fools these fellows must be, to bring such things with them." Without knowing what I was doing, I must have shaken my head disapprovingly. The inspection over, we sat for a short time in a hotel, then boarded the train. To my surprise, this flock of students started deferring to each other in the railway carriage. A wanted B to take this seat, B insisted on giving it up to C; and before they were through with this ceremonial the train started with a lurch, so that three or four of them promptly fell over. I was very annoyed again, and thought to myself: "Even the seats on trains they have to divide according to precedence...." Without knowing what I was doing, I must have shaken my head disapprovingly again. But one of that deferential group, I realized now, was Fan Ain-ong. And in addition to Fan, I am ashamed to say, were the revolutionary martyrs Chen Boping who was killed in battle in Anhui, and Ma Zonghan, who was murdered. There were one or two others as well, who were thrown into dark cells not to see the light of day till after the revolution, and who still bear the scars of their torture. But I did not know them; shaking my head I shipped them all to Tokyo. Though Xu Xilin had travelled on the same boat, he was not on this train, for he and his wife had landed at Kobe to go on by land.

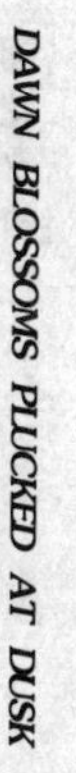

我想我那时摇头大约有两回，他们看见的不知道是那一回。让座时喧闹，检查时幽静，一定是在税关上的那一回了，试问爱农，果然是的。

“我真不懂你们带这东西做什么？是谁的？”

“还不是我们师母的？”他瞪着他多白的眼。

“到东京就要假装大脚，又何必带这东西呢？”

“谁知道呢？你问她去。”

到冬初，我们的景况更拮据了，然而还喝酒，讲笑话。忽然是武昌起义，接着是绍兴光复。第二天爱农就上城来，戴着农夫常用的毡帽，那笑容是从来没有见过的。

“老迅，我们今天不喝酒了。我要去看看光复的绍兴。我们同去。”

我们便到街上去走了一通，满眼是白旗。然而貌虽如此，内骨子是依旧的，因为还是几个旧乡绅所组织的军政府，什么铁路股东是行政司长，钱店掌

· I believed I must have shaken my head twice, and did not know which time they had noticed it, Since all was bustle and noise while they offered seats to each other, while all was quiet during the customs inspection, it must surely have been in the customhouse. When I questioned Ainong, I found this was the case.

"I really can't understand why you took such things with you. Whose were they?"

"They belonged to Mrs. Xu, of course." He fixed me with his eyes, which were mostly whites.

"In Tokyo she'd have to pretend to have big feet. So why take them?"

"How would I know? Ask her."

As winter approached we grew more hard up; still, we went on drinking and joking. Then suddenly came the Wuchang Uprising, and after that Shaoxing was liberated. The following day Ainong came to town in a felt cap of the type worn by peasants. I had never seen him with such a beaming face.

"Let's not drink today, Xun. I want to see liberated Shaoxing. Come on."

So we walk through the streets, and saw white flags everywhere. But though outwardly all was changed, beneath the surface all went on as before; for this was a military government organized by a few of the old-style gentry. The chief shareholder in the railway company was head of the administration, the moneylender had become director of the

柜是军械司长……。这军政府也到底不长久，几个少年一嚷，王金发带兵从杭州进来了，但即使不嚷或者也会来。他进来以后，也就被许多闲汉和新进的革命党所包围，大做王都督。在衙门里的人物，穿布衣来的，不上十天也大概换上皮袍子了，天气还并不冷。

我被摆在师范学校校长的饭碗旁边，王都督给了我校款二百元。爱农做监学，还是那件布袍子，但不大喝酒了，也很少有工夫谈闲天。他办事，兼教书，实在勤快得可以。

"情形还是不行，王金发他们。"一个去年听过我的讲义的少年来访问我，慷慨地说，"我们要办一种报来监督他们。不过发起人要借用先生的名字。还有一个是子英先生，一个是德清先生。为社会，我们知道你决不推却的。"

我答应他了。两天后便看见出报的传单，发起人诚然是三个。五天后便

arsenal....And this military government did not last long, for as soon as a few youngsters raised an outcry, Wang Jinfa came in with his troops from Hangzhou. In fact, he might have come even without the outcry. After his arrival, he was surrounded by a crowd of idlers and new members ofthe revolutionary party, and reigned supreme as Military Governor Wang. In less than ten days most of his men in the yamen, who had arrived in cotton clothes, were wearing fur-lined gowns although it was not yet cold.

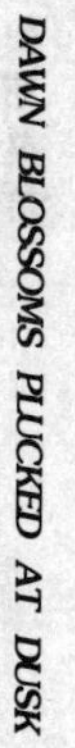

My new rice bowl was the job of principal of the normal school, and Governor Wang gave me two hundred dollars to run the school. Ainong was supervisor of studies. He still wore his cloth gown, but did not drink very much, and seldom had time to chat. Since he gave classes in addition to his administrative duties, he worked very hard indeed.

"Wang Jinfa and his lot are no good either," indignantly announced a young visitor who had attended my lectures the previous year. "We want to start a newspaper to keep a check on them. But we'll have to use your name, sir, as one of the sponsors. Another is Mr. Chen Ziying, and another is Mr. Sun Deqing. We know you won't refuse, since it's for the public good."

I gave my consent. Two days later I saw a leaflet announcing the appearance of this paper, and sure enough there were three sponsors. Five days

见报，开首便骂军政府和那里面的人员；此后是骂都督，都督的亲戚、同乡、姨太太……。

这样地骂了十多天，就有一种消息传到我的家里来，说都督因为你们诈取了他的钱，还骂他，要派人用手枪来打死你们了。

别人倒还不打紧，第一个着急的是我的母亲，叮嘱我不要再出去。但我还是照常走，并且说明，王金发是不来打死我们的，他虽然绿林大学出身，而杀人却不很轻易。况且我拿的是校款，这一点他还能明白的，不过说说罢了。

果然没有来杀。写信去要经费，又取了二百元。但仿佛有些怒意，同时传令道：再来要，没有了！

不过爱农得到了一种新消息，却使我很为难。原来所谓"诈取"者，并非指学校经费而言，是指另有送给报馆的一笔款。报纸上骂了几天之后，王金发便叫人送去了五百元。于是乎我们的少

later the newspaper came out. It began by denouncing the military government and its members, after which it denounced the governor and his relatives, fellow provincials and concubines....

After more than ten days of such abuse, wordcame to my house that because we had tricked money out of the governor and denounced him, he was going to send a gunman to shoot us.

Nobody took this seriously except my mother, who was very worried and begged me not to go out. I went as usual, however, explaining to her that Wang Jinfa would not be coming to shoot us; for although he came out of the bandits' school, he didn't kill people lightly. Besides, the money I took from his was to run the school — he should at least know that — he didn't mean what he said.

Sure enough, no one came to shoot us. When I wrote and asked for more funds, I received another two hundred dollars. But Governor Wang seemed to be rather offended, for he informed me: "This is the last time!"

Ainong heard some fresh news, however, which did upset me. The reference to "tricking" money had not meant the school funds but a separate sum given to the newspaper office. After the paper had come out for several days filled with abuse, Wang Jinfa sent a man there to pay them five hundred dollars. Then our youngsters held a meeting.

年们便开起会议来，第一个问题是：收不收？决议曰：收。第二个问题是：收了之后骂不骂？决议曰：骂。理由是：收钱之后，他是股东；股东不好，自然要骂。

我即刻到报馆去问这事的真假。都是真的。略说了几句不该收他钱的话，一个名为会计的便不高兴了，质问我道：——

"报馆为什么不收股本？"

"这不是股本……。"

"不是股本是什么？"

我就不再说下去了，这一点世故是早已知道的，倘我再说出连累我们的话来，他就会面斥我太爱惜不值钱的生命，不肯为社会牺牲，或者明天在报上就可以看见我怎样怕死发抖的记载。

然而事情很凑巧，季茀写信来催我往南京了。爱农也很赞成，但颇凄凉，说：——

The first question was: "Shall we accept this or not?"

The decision was "Accept it."

The second question was: "Shall we go on denouncing him after accepting this?"

The decision was: "We shall."

The reason was: "Once we have accepted his money, he becomes a shareholder; and if a shareholder behaves badly, of course we must denounce him."

I went straight to the newspaper office to find out whether this was true or not. It was. I reproached them mildly for accepting the governor's money, but the one called the accountant was offended.

"Why shouldn't a newspaper accept shares?" he demanded.

"These aren't shares. . . ."

"If they aren't shares, what are they?"

I did not say any more. I had enough experience of the world for that. If I had pointed out that this was involving us, he would have abused me for caring so much for my worthless life that I was unwilling to sacrifice myself for the public good; or the next day the paper might have carried an account of how I had trembled in my fear of death.

But then, by a fortunate coincidence, Xu Jifu sent me a letter urging me to go at once to Nangjing. Ainong was all in favour, though ex-

“这里又是那样，住不得。你快去罢……。”

我懂得他无声的话，决计往南京。先到都督府去辞职，自然照准，派来了一个拖鼻涕的接收员，我交出账目和余款一角又两铜元，不是校长了。后任是孔教会会长傅力臣。

报馆案是我到南京后两三个星期了结的，被一群兵们捣毁。子英在乡下，没有事；德清适值在城里，大腿上被刺了一尖刀。他大怒了。自然，这是很有些痛的，怪他不得。他大怒之后，脱下衣服，照了一张照片，以显示一寸来宽的刀伤，并且做一篇文章叙述情形，向各处分送，宣传军政府的横暴。我想，这种照片现在是大约未必还有人收藏着了，尺寸太小，刀伤缩小到几乎等于无，如果不加说明，看见的人一定以

tremely depressed as well.

"Things have grown so bad again, you can't stay here," he said. "You'd better leave at once...."

I understood what he left unsaid, and decided to go to Nanjing. First I went to the governor's yamen to tender my resignation, which was naturally accepted, then a snivelling functionary was sent to the school to take over. Having handed over the accounts and the ten cents and two coppers in hand, I ceased to be the principal. My successor was Fu Lichen, head of the Confucian League.

I heard the end of the newspaper affair two or three weeks after reaching Nanjing — the office had been smashed up by the soldiery. Since Chen Ziying was in the country, he was all right; but Sun Deqing, who happened to be in town, received a bayonet wound in his thigh. He flew into a fury. Of course, one could hardly blame him — it was rather painful. After his fury subsided, he took off his clothes and had a photograph taken to show the wound which was about an inch across; he also wrote an account of what had happened, which he circulated everywhere, to expose the tyranny of this military government. I doubt if anyone has kept that photograph. It was so small that the wound was practically invisible, and without an explanation anyone seeing it would he bound to take it for a nudist photograph of some rather eccentric and ro-

为是带些疯气的风流人物的裸体照片，倘遇见孙传芳大帅，还怕要被禁止的。

我从南京移到北京的时候，爱农的学监也被孔教会会长的校长设法去掉了。他又成了革命前的爱农。我想为他在北京寻一点小事做，这是他非常希望的，然而没有机会。他后来便到一个熟人的家里去寄食，也时时给我信，景况愈困穷，言辞也愈凄苦。终于又非走出这熟人的家不可，便在各处飘浮。不久，忽然从同乡那里得到一个消息，说他已经掉在水里，淹死了。

我疑心他是自杀。因为他是浮水的好手，不容易淹死的。

夜间独坐在会馆里，十分悲凉，又疑心这消息并不确，但无端又觉得这是极其可靠的，虽然并无证据。一点法子都没有，只做了四首诗，后来曾在一种日报上发表，现在是将要忘记完了。只记得一首里的六句，起首四句是："把酒论天下，先生小酒人，大圜犹酩酊，微醉

mantic fellow. Indeed, if it came to the notice of the warlord general Sun Chuanfang, it would very likely be banned.

By the time I moved from Nanjing to Peking, the principal who was head of the Confucian League had contrived to remove Ainong from his post as supervisor of studies. He was once more the Ainong of pre-revolutionary days. I wanted to find a small post for him in Peking, which was what he longed for, but there was no opening. Later he went to live on a friend, and I often heard from him. He grew poorer and poorer, and sounded more and more bitter. At last he was forced to leave this friend's house and drift from place to place. Before long I heard from a fellow provincial that he had fallen into the river and been drowned.

I suspected he had committed suicide. For he was an excellent swimmer: it would not be easy for him to drown.

At night, sitting in the hostel feeling thoroughly depressed, I doubted whether this news could be true; but somehow I still felt it must be reliable, although I had received no confirmation. There was nothing I could do but write four poems which were printed later in some paper, but which I have now nearly forgotten. All I can remember are six lines of one poem. The first four were:

> How often I discussed our times over wine
> With you who drank but little;

合沉沦。"中间忘掉两句,末了是"旧朋云散尽,余亦等轻尘。"

后来我回故乡去,才知道一些较为详细的事。爱农先是什么事也没得做,因为大家讨厌他。他很困难,但还喝酒,是朋友请他的。他已经很少和人们来往,常见的只剩下几个后来认识的较为年青的人了,然而他们似乎也不愿意多听他的牢骚,以为不如讲笑话有趣。

"也许明天就收到一个电报,拆开来一看,是鲁迅来叫我的。"他时常这样说。

一天,几个新的朋友约他坐船去看戏,回来已过夜半,又是大风雨,他醉着,却偏要到船舷上去小解。大家劝阻他,也不听,自己说是不会掉下去的。但他掉下去了,虽然能浮水,却从此不起来。

第二天打捞尸体,是在菱荡里找到

In a world blind drunk

A mere tippler might well drown....

The two lines in the middle have slipped my memory, but the last two were:

Like scattering clouds my friends have gone,

And I am but a grain of dust in the wind.

Later, when I went home, I learned more details of the story. First, Ainong could find no work of any description, because everybody disliked him. He was very hard up indeed, but he went on drinking whenever friends treated him. He had very little to do with other people by this time, and the only ones he saw much of were a few rather young men he had got to know afterwards; but they did not want to hear his complants all the time — they liked his jokes better.

"I may get a telegram tomorrow." he used to say. "When I open it, I'll find Lu Xun has sent for me."

One day, a few new friends invited him to go by boat to watch an opera. It was after midnight by the time they started back, and there was high wind and rain. He was drunk, yet he insisted on standing on the bulwarks. And when his friends protested, he would not listen to them. He assured them he could not fall. Fall he did, though, and although he could swim he did not come to the surface.

The next day they recovered his body. They

的，直立着。

我至今不明白他究竟是失足还是自杀。

他死后一无所有，遗下一个幼女和他的夫人。有几个人想集一点钱作他女孩将来的学费的基金，因为一经提议，即有族人来争这笔款的保管权，——其实还没有这笔款，大家觉得无聊，便无形消散了。

现在不知他唯一的女儿景况如何？倘在上学，中学已该毕业了罢。

十一月十八日。

found him standing upright in a creek where water chestnuts grew.

To this day I do not know whether he lost his balance or committed suicide.

He had no money at all when he died, but he left behind a widow with a young daughter. Some people thought of starting a fund for his daughter's future schooling; but as soon as this was proposed, various members of his clan started squabbling as to who should control this sum, although it had not yet been collected. Then everyone was so disgusted that the scheme just came to nothing.

I wonder how his only daughter is faring now? If she is studying, she ought to have graduated from secondary school by this time.

November 18

后记

我在第三篇讲《二十四孝》的开头，说北京恐吓小孩的“马虎子”应作“麻胡子”，是指麻叔谋，而且以他为胡人。现在知道是错了，“胡”应作“祜”，是叔谋之名，见唐人李济翁做的《资暇集》卷下，题云《非麻胡》原文如次：——

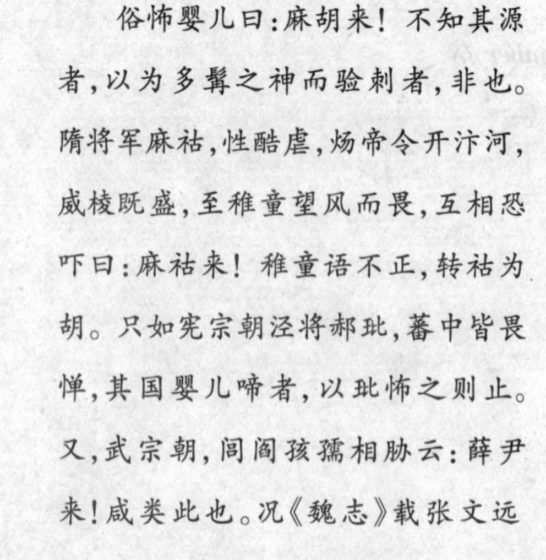

俗怖婴儿曰：麻胡来！不知其源者，以为多髯之神而验刺者，非也。隋将军麻祜，性酷虐，炀帝令开汴河，威棱既盛，至稚童望风而畏，互相恐吓曰：麻祜来！稚童语不正，转祜为胡。只如宪宗朝泾将郝玭，蕃中皆畏惮，其国婴儿啼者，以玭怖之则止。又，武宗朝，闾阎孩孺相胁云：薛尹来！咸类此也。况《魏志》载张文远

Postscript

At the start of my third essay on *The Twenty-Four Acts of Filial Piety*, I said that the term *Ma Huzi* used in Peking to frighten children should be "Ma the Hun" because it referred to Ma Shumou, whom I took to be a Hun, I now find I was wrong. Hu was General Ma Shumou's first name. This appears in *Notes for Idle Moments* by Li Jiweng of the Tang Dynasty. The seciton entitled "Refuting the View That Ma Shumou Was a Hun" reads as follows:

> "Common people frighten children by saying, 'Ma Huzi is coming!' Those not knowing the origin of this saying imagine Ma as a god with a big beard who is a harsh investigator of people's crimes; but this is wrong. There was a stern, cruel general of Sui called Ma Hu, to whom Emperor Yang Di entrusted the task of building the Grand Canal at Bianliang. So powerful was he that even children stood in awe of him and would frighten each other by saying, 'Ma Huzi is coming!' In their childish prattle the Hu changed into Hun.
>
> This is just like the case of General Hao Pin of the prefecture of Jing in the reign of Emperor Xian Zong, who was so feared by the barbarians that they stopped their children from crying by scaring them with his name. Again, in the time of Emperor Wu Zong, village children would threaten each other, 'Prefect Xue is coming!' Three are various similar instances, as is proved by the accountin the *Wei Records* of Zhang Liao

辽来之明证乎？（原注：麻祜庙在睢阳。鄜方节度李丕即其后。丕为重建碑。）

原来我的识见，就正和唐朝的“不知其源者”相同，贻讥于千载之前，真是咎有应得，只好苦笑。但又不知麻祜庙碑或碑文，现今尚在睢阳或存于方志中否？倘在，我们当可以看见和小说《开河记》所载相反的他的功业。

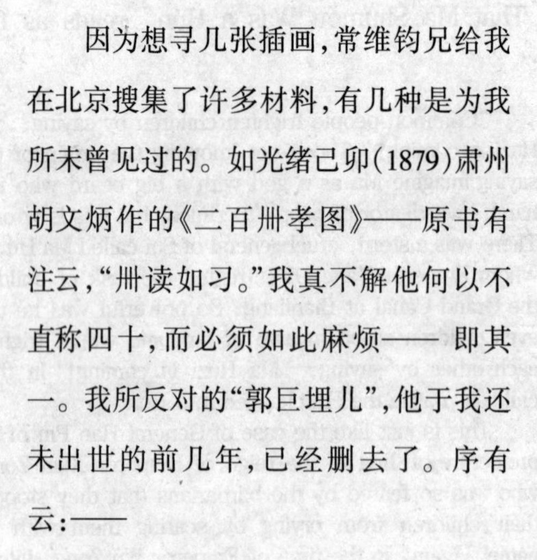

因为想寻几张插画，常维钧兄给我在北京搜集了许多材料，有几种是为我所未曾见过的。如光绪己卯(1879)肃州胡文炳作的《二百卌孝图》——原书有注云，“卌读如习。”我真不解他何以不直称四十，而必须如此麻烦——即其一。我所反对的“郭巨埋儿”，他于我还未出世的前几年，已经删去了。序有云：——

being invoked as a bogeyman." (Author's note: Ma Hu's Temple is in Suiyang. Li Pi, Governor of Fufang, who was his descendant, had a new tablet erected and inscribed there.)

So, I, in my understanding, was just like "Those not knowing the origin of this saying" in the Tang Dynasty, and I truly deserved to be jeered at by someone a thousand years ago. All I can do is laugh wryly. I do not know whether this tablet is still at Ma Hu's Temple in Suiyang or whether the inscription has been kept in the local records or not. If they still exist, we should be able to see his real achievements, which would be the opposite of those described in the story *Record of the Construction of the Canal*.

Because I wanted to find a few illustration, Mr. Chang Weijun collected a wealth of material for me in Peking, among it a few books which I had never seen. These included *Picture-Book of Two Hundred and Forty Filial Acts* by Hu Wenbing of Suzhou, published in 1879, the fifth year of Guang Xu. The word "forty" was written 卌 and there was a note to the effect that this should be pronounced *xi*. Why he went to such trouble instead of simply writing "forty" passes my understanding. As to that story to which I objected about Guo Ju burying his child alive, he had already cut it a few years before I was born. The preface says:

……坊间所刻《二十四孝》,善矣。然其中郭巨埋儿一事,揆之天理人情,殊不可以训。……炳窃不自量,妄为编辑。凡矫枉过正而刻意求名者,概从割爱;惟择其事之不诡于正,而人人可为者,类为六门。……

这位肃州胡老先生的勇决,委实令我佩服了。但这种意见,恐怕是怀抱者不乏其人,而且由来已久的,不过大抵不敢毅然删改,笔之于书。如同治十一年(1872)刻的《百孝图》,前有纪常郑绩序,就说:

……况迩来世风日下,沿习浇漓,不知孝出天性自然,反以孝作另成一事。且择古人投炉埋儿为忍心害理,指割股抽肠为损亲遗体。殊未审孝只在乎心,不在乎迹。尽孝无定形,行孝无定事。古之孝者非在今所宜,今之孝者难泥古之事。因此时此地不同,而其人其事各异,求其所以尽孝之心则一也。子夏曰:事父母能

"... *The Twenty-Four Acts of Filial Piety* brought out by the publishers is an excellent book, but its account of Guo Ju burying his son is not a good example to follow, according neither with reason nor human feeling.... I have rashly taken it upon myself to bring out a new edition, weeding out all those stories which aim at winning a name by exceeding proper limits, and choosing only which do not deviate from the rules of propriety and which can be taken as examples by all. These I have grouped into six categories."

The courage of this old Mr. Hu from Suzhou is certainly admirable. But I think many people must have shared his views, from way back too, only probably lacked the courage to make bold cuts or commit their views to writing. Take for instance The *Picture-Book of a Hundred Filial Acts* published in 1872, the eleventh year of Tong Zhi, with a preface by Zheng Ji (alias Zheng Jichang) which says:

"...Now that morality is going to the dogs and the old customs are being undermined, forgetting that filial piety is human nature people regard it as something quite apart. They pick out stories of men of bygone days throwing themselves into furnaces or burying children alive and dub them as cruel and irrational, or accuse those who cut flesh from their things or disembowelled themselves of injurng the body given them by their parents. They do not realize that filial piety is a matter of feeling, not of outward forms. It has no fixed forms, no fixed observances. The filial piety of ancient times may not suit present needs; we today can hardly model ourselves on the ancients. For thetime and place have changed, and different people will perform different deeds although all alike wish to be filial. Zi Xia said that a man should put his whole strength into serving his parents. So if people asked Confucius how to be filial

竭其力。故孔门问孝,所答何尝有同然乎?……

则同治年间就有人以埋儿等事为“忍心害理”,灼然可知。至于这一位“纪常郑绩”先生的意思,我却还是不大懂,或者像是说:这些事现在可以不必学,但也不必说他错。

这部《百孝图》的起源有点特别,是因为见了“粤东颜子”的《百美新咏》而作的。人重色而己重孝,卫道之盛心可谓至矣。虽然是“会稽俞葆真兰浦编辑”,与不佞有同乡之谊,——但我还只得老实说:不大高明。例如木兰从军的出典,他注云:“隋史”。这样名目的书,现今是没有的;倘是《隋书》,那里面又没有木兰从军的事。

而中华民国九年(1920),上海的书店却偏偏将它用石印翻印了,书名的前后各添了两个字:《男女百孝图全传》。

his answer would vary according to different cases...."

From this it is clear that in the reign of Tong Zhi some people considered such acts as burying a child alive as "cruel and irrational." As for this Mr. Zheng Ji's personal views, I am not too clear about them. He may have meant that we need not follow such old examples but at the same time need not consider them wrong.

The origin of this *Picture-Book of a Hundred Filial Acts* is rather unusual: it was the result of reading *New Poems on a Hundred Beauties* by a man called Yan from eastern Guangdong. Whereas Yan laid stress on female charm, the author laid stess on filial piety, showing splended zeal in championing morality. However, though this book was complied by Yu Baozhen (alias Yu Lanpu) of Kuaiji, in other words, a man from my own district, I still have to say frankly that it is not up to much. For example, in a note to the story about Mulan joining the army in her father's place, he ascribed it to the "Sui Shi" (Sui Dynasty History.) No book of this name exists. If he meant the *Sui Shu* (*Records of Sui*), that work has no reference to Mulan joining the army.

Still this book was reprinted in lithorgraphic edition by a Shanghai publisher in 1920, the ninth year of the republic, under the amplified title *Complete Edition of the Picture-Book of a Hundred Fil-*

第一叶上还有一行小字道：家庭教育的好模范。又加了一篇“吴下大错王鼎谨识”的序，开首先发同治年间“纪常郑绩”先生一流的感慨：——

> 嘅自欧化东渐，海内承学之士，嚣嚣然侈谈自由平等之说，致道德日就沦胥，人心日益浇漓，寡廉鲜耻，无所不为，侥幸行险，人思幸进，求所谓砥砺廉隅，束身自爱者，世不多睹焉。……起观斯世之忍心害理，几全如陈叔宝之无心肝。长此滔滔，伊何底止？……

其实陈叔宝模胡到好像“全无心肝”，或者有之，若拉他来配“忍心害理”，却未免有些冤枉。这是有几个人以评“郭巨埋儿”和“李娥投炉”的事的。

至于人心，有几点确也似乎正在浇漓起来。自从《男女之秘密》、《男女交合新论》出现后，上海就很有些书名喜欢用“男女”二字冠首。现在是连“以正人心而厚风俗”的《百孝图》上也加上

ial Acts by Men and Women. And on the first page, in small print, were the words: Good models for family education. There was also an additional preface by a certain Wang Ding (alias Wang Dacuo) of Suzhou, which started off with a lament similaar to the views of Mr. Zheng Ji of the Tong Zhi reign:

> "Ever since European influence spread east, scholars within the Four Seas have been advocating freedom and equality, so that morality has daily declined and men's hearts are becoming daily more depraved, unscrupulous and shameless, making them do all manner of evil, running risks and trusting to luck to get ahead. Few indeed are the men of integrity who have scruples and will not lower themselves.... I see that this world's irrational cruelty is well-nigh as bad as the heartlessness of Chen Shubao. If this tendency goes unchecked, what will our end be?..."

Chen Shubao may actually have been so stupid that he seemed completely "heartless," but it is rather unfair to drag him in as an example of irrational cruelty, when such terms had been used by others to describe Guo Ju's burying his son and Li E throwing herself into a furnace.

In some ways, however, people's hearts do seem to be growing more depraved. Ever since the publication of *Secrets Between Men and Women* and *New Treatise on intercourse Between Men and Women*, many books published in Shanghai use "men and women" in their titles. So now these words have been added even to the *Picture Book of a Hundred Filial Acts* which was published to "rec-

了。这大概为因不满于《百美新咏》而教孝的“会稽俞葆真兰浦”先生所不及料的罢。

从说“百行之先”的孝而忽然拉到“男女”上去,仿佛也近乎不庄重,——浇漓。但我总还想趁便说几句,——自然竭力来减省。

我们中国人即使对于“百行之先”,我敢说,也未必就不想到男女上去的。太平无事,闲人很多,偶有“杀身成仁舍生取义”的,本人也许忙得不暇检点,而活着的旁观者总会加以绵密的研究。曹娥的投江觅父,淹死后抱父尸出,是载在正史,很有许多人知道的。但这一个“抱”字却发生过问题。

我幼小时候,在故乡曾经听到老年人这样讲:——

“……死了的曹娥,和她父亲的尸体,最初是面对面抱着浮上来的。然而过往行人看见的都发笑了,说:哈哈!这么一个年青姑娘抱着这么一个老

tify men's minds and improve their morals." This is probably something never expected by Mr. Yu Baozhen of Kuaiji, who because of his dissatisfaction with the *New Poems on a Hundred Beauties* preached filial piety.

To depart suddenly from filial piety, "the foremost of all virtues," to drag in "men and women" may seem rather frivolous if not depraved. Still, I would like to take this chance to say a few words on this subject. Of course, I shall try to be brief.

We Chinese, I dare say, even when it comes to "the foremost of all virtues, may sometimes start thinking of men and women too. The world is at peace, so idle people abound. Occasionally some "kill themselves for a noble cause" and may be too busy themselves to bother about other matters, but onlookers who remain alive can always carry out detailed researches. Official histories relate, and it is quite commonly known, that Cao E jumped into the river to look for her father, and after drowning herself still carried his corpse out. The problem is: *How* did she carry his corpse?

When I was small, I heard elders in my hometown explain it this way:

"...At first, the dead Cao E and her father's corpse floated up to the surface with her clasping him, face to face. But passers-by seeing this laughed and said: 'Look, such a young girl with her

头子！于是那两个死尸又沉下去了；停了一刻又浮起来，这回是背对背的负着。”

好！在礼义之邦里，连一个年幼——呜呼，“娥年十四”而已——的死孝女要和死父亲一同浮出，也有这么艰难！

我检查《百孝图》和《二百卌孝图》，画师都很聪明，所画的是曹娥还未跳入江中，只在江干啼哭。但吴友如画的《女二十四孝图》(1892)却正是两尸一同浮出的这一幕，而且也正画作“背对背”，如第一图的上方。我想，他大约也知道我所听到的那故事的。还有《后二十四孝图说》，也是吴友如画，也有曹娥，则画作正在投江的情状，如第一图下。

就我现今所见的教孝的图说而言，古今颇有许多遇盗，遇虎，遇火，遇风的孝子，那应付的方法，十之九是“哭”和“拜”。

arms round such an old man!' Then the two corpses sank back into the water. After a little they floated up again, this time back to back"

Fine! According to the records, "E was only fourteen." But in this realm of propriety and righteousness, even for so young a dead filial daughter to float up from the water with her dead father is very, very hard.

I looked up the *Picture-Book of a Hundred Filial Acts* and *Picture-Book of Two Hundred and Forty Filial Acts*. In both cases the artists were clever: they had only drawn Cao E weeping on the bank before jumping into the river. But the 1892 edition of *The Picture-Book of Twenty-Four Filial Women* illustrated by Wu Youru showed the scene of the two corpses floating up, and he had made them "back to back" as we see in the uppermost of the first illustration. I expect he had heard the same story that I did. Then there is the *Supplementary Picture-Book of Twenty-Four Filial Acts* also illustrated by Wu Youru, in which Cao E is again presented, this time in the act of plunging into the river, as we see in the lower of the first illustration.

A great many of the illustrated stories preaching filial piety which I have seen show filial sons through the ages up against brigands, tigers or hurricanes, and nine times out of ten their way of coping with the situation is "weeping" and "kowtowing."

後二十四孝圖說
曹娥投江
尋父屍
三

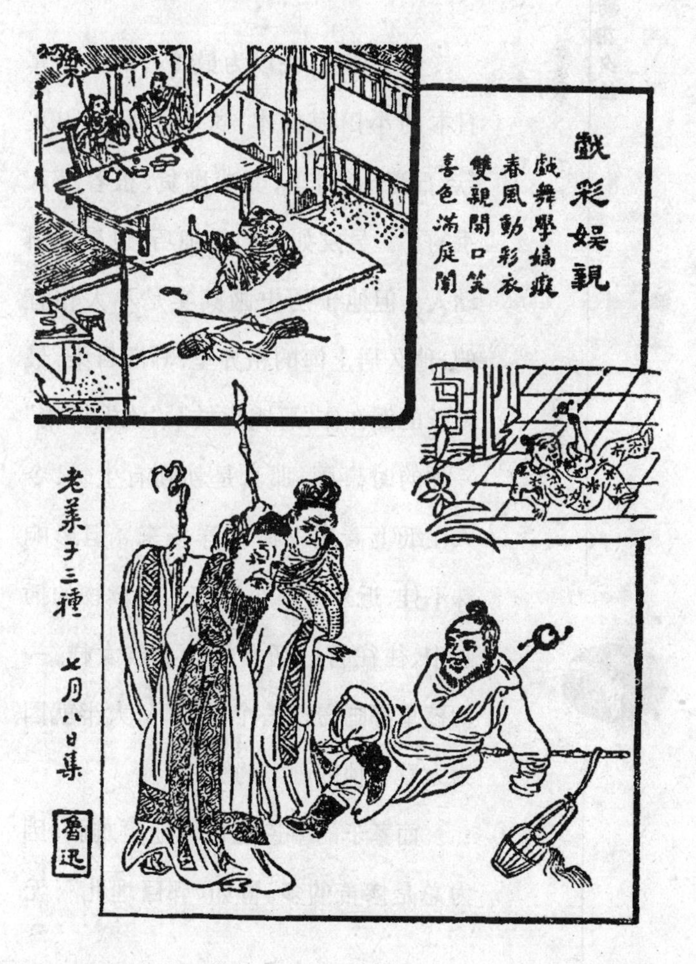
戲彩娛親
戲舞學嬌癡
春風動彩衣
雙親開口笑
喜色滿庭闈
老莱子三種
七月八日集
魯迅

中国的哭和拜,什么时候才完呢?

至于画法,我以为最简古的倒要算日本的小田海仙本,这本子早已印入《点石斋丛画》里,变成国货,很容易入手的了。吴友如画的最细巧,也最能引动人。但他于历史画其实是不大相宜的;他久居上海的租界里,耳濡目染,最擅长的倒在作“恶鸨虐妓”,“流氓拆梢”一类的时事画,那真是勃勃有生气,令人在纸上看出上海的洋场来。但影响殊不佳,近来许多小说和儿童读物的插画中,往往将一切女性画成妓女样,一切孩童都画得像一个小流氓,大半就因为太看了他的画本的缘故。

而孝子的事迹也比较地更难画,因为总是惨苦的多。譬如“郭巨埋儿”,无

When will we stop "weeping" and "kowtowing" in China?

As far as draughtsmanship is concerned, I think the simplest and most classical style is that of the Japanese edition by Oda Umisen. Having already been incorporated into *Paintings Collected by Dianshizhai*, this has become a Chinese product and so is very easy to get hold of. Wu Youru's illustrations, being the most meticulous, are also the most engaging. But in point of fact he was not too well fitted to draw historical subjects. For he was not too well fitted to draw historical subjects. For he was so thoroughly imbued with what he had seen and heard in the course of his long residence in the International Settlement in Shanghai that what he really excelled at was contemporary scenes such as "A Fierce Bawd Abuses a Prostitute" or "A Hooligan Makes Advances to a Woman." Such pictures are so full of vigour and life that they conjure up before us the International Settlement in Shanghai. However, Wu's influence was deplorable. You will find that in the illustrations of many recent novels or children's books all the women are drawn like prostitutes, all thechildren like young hooligans, and this is very largely the result of the artists seeing too many of his illustration.

And stories about filial sons are even more difficult to illustrate, because most of them are so

论如何总难以画到引得孩子眉飞色舞，自愿躺到坑里去。还有“尝粪心忧”，也不容易引人入胜。还有老莱子的“戏彩娱亲”，题诗上虽说“喜色满庭帏”，而图画上却绝少有有趣的家庭的气息。

我现在选取了三种不同的标本，合成第二图。上方的是《百孝图》中的一部分，“陈村何云梯”画的，画的是“取水上堂诈跌卧地作婴儿啼”这一段。也带出“双亲开口笑”来。中间的一小块是我从“直北李锡彤”画的《二十四孝图诗合刊》上描下来的，画的是“著五色斑斓之衣为婴儿戏于亲侧”这一段；手里捏着“摇咕咚”，就是“婴儿戏”这三个字的点题。但大约李先生觉得一个高大的老头子玩这样的把戏究竟不像样，将他的身子竭力收缩，画成一个有胡子的小孩子了。然而仍然无趣。至于线的错误和缺少，那是不能怪作者的，也不能

sad. Take for instance the story "Guo Ju Buries His Son." No matter how, you can hardly make a picture that will induce children to lay themselves down eagerly in a pit. And the story "Tasting Faeces with an Anxious Heart" is hardly likely to make much appeal either. Again, in the tale about "Old Lai Zi Amuses His Parents," although the verse appended to it says "the whole household was filled with joy," the illustrations have very little in them to suggest a happy family atmosphere.

I have chosen three different examples for the second page of illustration. The scene at the top, from *The Picture-Book of a Hundred Filial Acts*, was drawn by He Yunti of Chencun. It shows Old Lai Zi pretending to fall while carrying water to the hall and crying like a baby on the ground, and also shows his parents laughing. The middle scene I copied myself from *Pictures and Poems of Twenty-Four Filial Acts* illustrated by Li Xitong of northern Zhili. It shows Old Lai Zi in multicoloured garments playing childish pranks in front of his parents. The rattle in his hand brings out the fact that he is pretending to be a baby. Probably, however, this Mr. Li felt that it looked too ridiculous for a fully grown old man to play such pranks, so he did his best to cut Old Lai Zi down in size, finally drawing a small child with a beard. Even so, it makes no appeal. As for the mistakes and gaps in the lines, they are neither the fault of the artist nor mine as

埋怨我，只能去骂刻工。查这刻工当前清同治十二年(1873)时，是在“山东省布政司街南首路西鸿文堂刻字处”。下方的是“民国壬戌”(1922)慎独山房刻本，无画人姓名，但是双料画法，一面“诈跌卧地”，一面“为婴儿戏”，将两件事合起来，而将“斑斓之衣”忘却了。吴友如画的一本，也合两事为一，也忘了斑斓之衣，只是老莱子比较的胖一些，且绾着双丫髻，——不过还是无趣味。

人说，讽刺和冷嘲只隔一张纸，我以为有趣和肉麻也一样。孩子对父母撒娇可以看得有趣，若是成人，便未免有些不顺眼。放达的夫妻在人面前的互相爱怜的态度，有时略一跨出有趣的界线，也容易变为肉麻。老莱子的作态的图，正无怪谁也画不好。像这些图画上似的家庭里，我是一天也住不舒服的，你看这样一位七十多岁的老太爷整年假惺惺地玩着一个“摇咕咚”。

copyist; one can only blame the engraver who in 1873, the twelfth year of Tong Zhi in the Qing Dynasty, worked in the Hongwentang Printing Shop on the west side of the southern end of Buzhengsi Street in the Province of Shandong. The bottom picture on this page was printed by the Shendushanfang Shop in 1922, the eleventh year of the republic, without giving the artist's name. The illustration contains two episodes — pretending to fall and playing pranks like a baby — but leaves out the "multicoloured garments." Wu Youru's illustration also combines both episodes; and he has also left out the multicoloured garments, but although his Old Lai Zi is plumper and has his hair in two knots — he still looks unattractive.

It has been said that the difference between satire and invective is only paper-thin, and I think the same applies to winsomeness and mawkishness. A child playing pranks before its parents can be winsome, but if a grown man does this it cannot but be distasteful. A careless married couple displaying their mutual fondness in public can easily become embarrassing if they slightly overstep the bounds of what is amusing. It is no wonder, then, that no one could draw a good picture of Old Lai Zi playing pranks. I could not be comfortable, even for a day, living in a family such as these pictures show. Just think. How can this old gentleman in his seventies spend all his time playing hypocritically with a rat-

汉朝人在宫殿和墓前的石室里，多喜欢绘画或雕刻古来的帝王、孔子弟子、列士、列女、孝子之类的图。宫殿当然一椽不存了；石室却偶然还有，而最完全的是山东嘉祥县的武氏石室。我仿佛记得那上面就刻着老莱子的故事。但现在手头既没有拓本，也没有《金石萃编》，不能查考了；否则，将现时的和约一千八百年前的图画比较起来，也是一种颇有趣味的事。

关于老莱子的，《百孝图》上还有这样的一段：——

……莱子又有弄雏娱亲之事：尝弄雏于双亲之侧，欲亲之喜。（原注：《高士传》。）

谁做的《高士传》呢？嵇康的，还是皇甫谧的？也还是手头没有书，无从查考。只在新近因为白得了一个月的薪水，这才发狠买来的《太平御览》上查了

tle?

People of the Han Dynasty liked to have paintings or carved reliefs of rulers of old, disciples of Confucius, eminent scholars and ladies and filial sons in their palaces or the stone chambers before their tombs. Of course none of those palaces are left today, but occasionally such stone chambers can be seen. The one best preserved is the Wu family stone chamber in Jiaxiang County, Shandong. I seem to remember that it has a relief depicting the story of Old Lai Zi. But since I do not have the rubbings with me, and have no copy of the book *Collected Inscriptions on Stone and Metal* either, I cannot verify this. Otherwise it would be most interesting to compare modern illustrations with those done about eighteen hundred years ago.

Regarding Old Lai Zi's story, there is the following account in the *Picture-Book of a Hundred Filial Acts*:

> "... Old Lai Zi also played with a chu (雏) to amuse his parents. He romped with this at their side to divert them." (Author's note: from *Lives of Lofty Character*.)

Whose *Lives of Lofty Characters* did he mean? That by Ji Kang? Or that by Huangfu Mi? Again I had no books where I could look this up. Recently, however, on receiving one extra month's pay I decided to buy a set of *The Imperial Encyclopedia of*

一通，到底查不着，倘不是我粗心，那就是出于别的唐宋人的类书里的了。但这也没有什么大关系。我所觉得特别的，是文中的那“雏”字。

我想，这“雏”未必一定是小禽鸟。孩子们喜欢弄来玩耍的，用泥和绸或布做成的人形，日本也叫 Hina，写作“雏”。他们那里往往存留中国的古语；而老莱子在父母面前弄孩子的玩具，也比弄小禽鸟更自然。所以英语的 Doll，即我们现在称为“洋囡囡”或“泥人儿”，而文字上只好写作“傀儡”的，说不定古人就称“雏”，后来中绝，便只残存于日本了。但这不过是我一时的臆测，此外也并无什么坚实的凭证。

这弄雏的事，似乎也还没有人画过图。

我所搜集的另一批，是内有“无常”的画像的书籍。一曰《玉历钞传警世》（或无下二字），一曰《玉历至宝钞》（或作编）。其实是两种都差不多的。关于

the Taiping Era. But on looking through this, I still failed to find the source. So either I did not look carefully enough, or else the anecdote must come from some other Tang or Song book. Not that this really matters. What struck me as interesting in the text was the word *chu*.

It seems to me that *chu* here may not mean a fledgeling. Dolls made of clay, silk or cloth as children's toys are called *hina* in Japanese, and the character for this is the same as *chu*. They have retained not a few old Chinese characters over there; and for Old Lai Zi to play with a child's toy before his parents sounds more natural than playing with a little bird. What in English is called a "doll" we in China today call a *yang-nan-nan* or *nirenr* but we have to write this with the characters *kui-lei* (puppet). So perhaps our ancestors called it *chu* but later this word was lost and only preserved in Japan. However, this is just my hypothesis for the time being. I have not as yet found substantial evidence.

It seems that nobody ever drew a picture of Old Lai Zi playing with a doll.

Another set of books I collected was those withpictures of Wu Chang or Life-Is-Transient. One is *Cautionary Records of the Jade Calendar* (or the word "cautionary" may be omitted), another is *Most Treasured Records of the Jade Calendar*. Actually the contents are almost identical. Regarding

搜集的事，我首先仍要感谢常维钧兄，他寄给我北京龙光斋本，又鉴光斋本；天津思过斋本，又石印局本；南京李光明庄本。其次是章矛尘兄，给我杭州玛瑙经房本，绍兴许广记本，最近石印本。又其次是我自己，得到广州宝经阁本，又翰元楼本。

这些《玉历》，有繁简两种，是和我的前言相符的。但我调查了一切无常的画像之后，却恐慌起来了。因为书上的“活无常”是花袍、纱帽、背后插刀；而拿算盘，戴高帽子的却是“死有分”！虽然面貌有凶恶和和善之别，脚下有草鞋和布(?)鞋之殊，也不过画工偶然的随便，而最关紧要的题字，则全体一致，曰：“死有分”。呜呼，这明明是专在和我为难。

然而我还不能心服。一者因为这些书都不是我幼小时候所见的那一部，二者因为我还确信我的记忆并没有错。

the collecting of these books I must first of all thank Mr. Chang Weijun who sent me the Longguangzhai and Jianguangzhai editions printed in Peking, the Siguozhai and Lithorgraphic Printing Shop editions printed in Tianjin, and the Liguangmingzhuang edition printed in Nangjing. Next my thanks are due to Mr. Zhang Maochen who gave me the Manaojingfang edition printed in Hangzhou, the Xuguangji edition printed in Shaoxing, and the most recent lithographic edition. Then I myself procured the Baojingge edition printed in Guangzhou and the Hanyuanlou edition.

There are two kinds of these *Jade Calendars*, one comprehensive and the other briefer, as I stated earlier. But a study of all the pictures of Wu Chang started me worrying. For in these books Wu Chang or Life-Is-Transient wears a gaudy robe and gauze headdress, and has a sword fastened on his back; while the ghost with the abacus and tall conical hat is Death-Is-Predestined! Though their faces may be fierce or kind, and they may be wearing straw sandals or cloth (?) shoes, these discrepancies merely depend on the whim of the artist; but the important thing, which all have in common, is that they are called Death-Is-Predestined. Alas, this wasclearly done to make things awkward for me.

Still I am not convinced. In the first place, none of these books is the edition I saw in my childhood; in the second, I still believe that my memory

不过撕下一叶来做插画的企图,却被无声无臭地打得粉碎了。只得选取标本各一——南京本的死有分和广州本的活无常——之外,还自己动手,添画一个我所记得的目连戏或迎神赛会中的“活无常”来塞责,如第三图上方。好在我并非画家,虽然太不高明,读者也许不至于嗔责罢。先前想不到后来,曾经对于吴友如先生辈颇说过几句蹊跷话,不料曾几何时,即须自己出丑了,现在就预先辩解几句在这里存案。但是,如果无效,那也只好直抄徐(印世昌)大总统的哲学:听其自然。

还有不能心服的事,是我觉得虽是宣传《玉历》的诸公,于阴间的事情其实也不大了然。例如一个人初死时的情状,那图像就分成两派。一派是只来一位手执钢叉的鬼卒,叫作“勾魂使者”,此外什么都没有;一派是一个马面,两个无常——阳无常和阴无常——而并非活无常和死有分。倘说,那两个就是

is not at fault. However, my scheme of tearing off a single page to serve as an illustration was quietly but completely frustrated. All I could do was to pick an example of each — one Death-Is-Predestined from a Nanjing edition and one Life-Is-Transient from a Guangzhou edition, in addition I had to set to work myself to sketch by way of substitute the Life-Is-Transient I remembered from Maudgalyaymmana dramas or temple fairs, for the upper part of the third page of illustrations. Luckily I am not a professional artist, so although the sketch is not too good, readers should not be too critical. Lacking foresight I commented disrespectfully on Mr. Wu Youru and his confrères, little thinking I should have to make a fool of myself so shortly after. So I am saying a few words of apology here in advance. But if my apology is not accepted, I can only imitate President Xu Shichang's philosophy: let things take their natural course.

Another thing of which I am not convinced is this: Do those gentlemen who boost the *Jade Calendar* really have a clear understanding of the nether regions? For example, there are two kinds of illustrations of the scene at a man's death; one shows simply a ghost guard armed with a steel trident, known as the Sum-moner of Ghosts, and nobody else; one shows a horse-faced devil and two Wu Changs — Wu Chang of the world of men and Wu Chang of the shades — but these are not Life-Is-

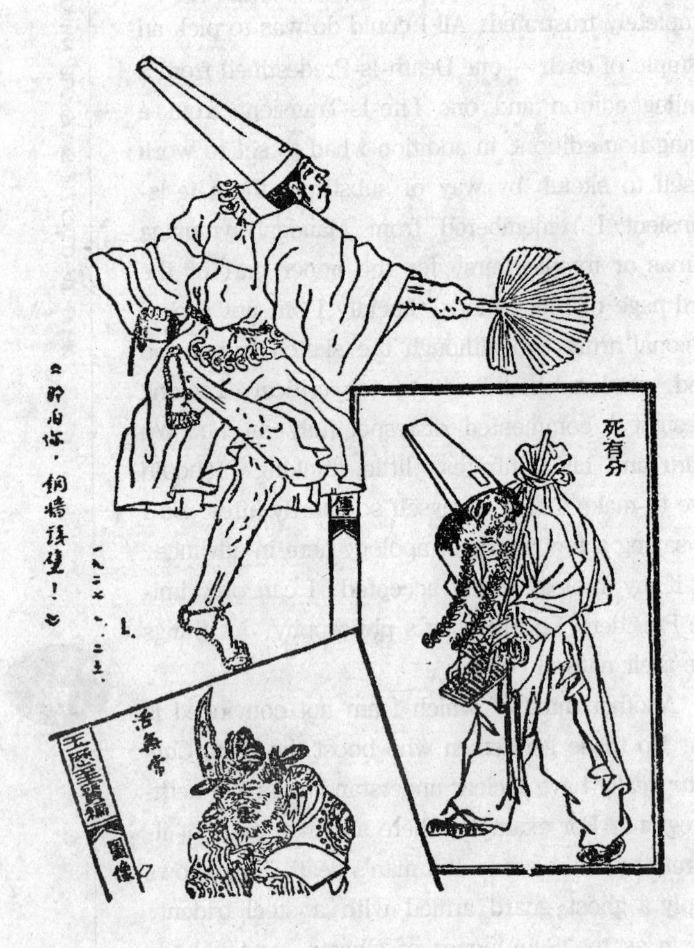

死有分
傳
活無常
玉歷至寶編
圖像
◎那怕你，銅墻鐵壁！◎
一九二六，六，二三。
L.

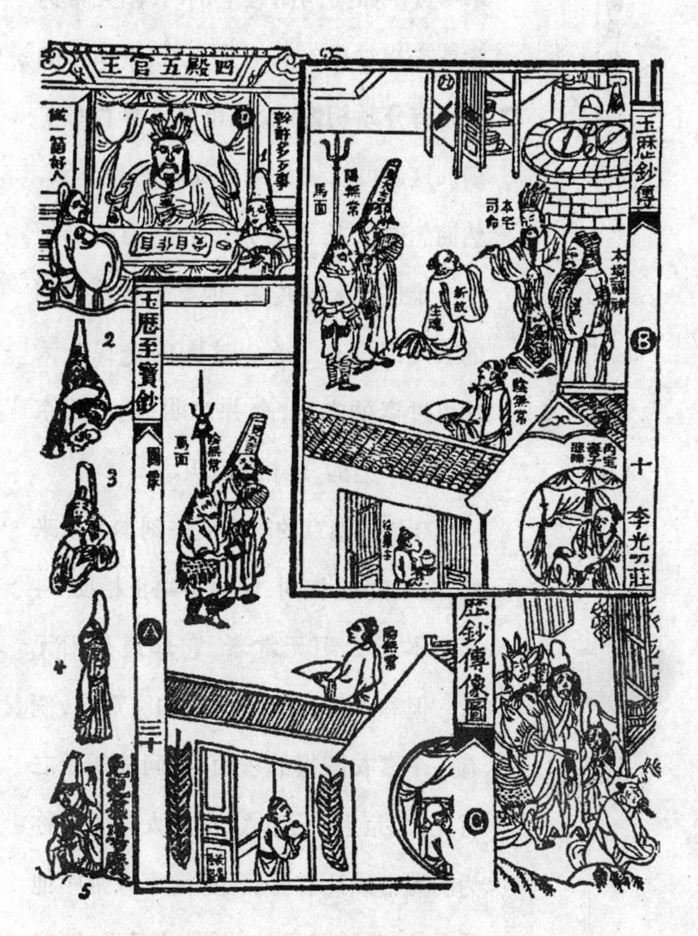

四殿五官王
玉歷鈔傳
玉歷至寶鈔
歷鈔傳像圖
陽無常
馬面
本宅司命
本境福神
新故生魂
陰無常

活无常和死有分罢,则和单个的画像又不一致。如第四图版上的A,阳无常何尝是花袍纱帽?只有阴无常却和单画的死有分颇相像的,但也放下算盘拿了扇。这还可以说大约因为其时是夏天,然而怎么又长了那么长的络腮胡子了呢?难道夏天时疫多,他竟忙得连修刮的工夫都没有了么?这图的来源是天津思过斋的本子,合并声明;还有北京和广州本上的,也相差无几。

B是从南京的李光明庄刻本上取来的,图画和A相同,而题字则正相反了:天津本指为阴无常者,它却道是阳无常。但和我的主张是一致的。那么,倘有一个素衣高帽的东西,不问他胡子之有无,北京人、天津人、广州人只管去称为阴无常或死有分,我和南京人则叫他活无常,各随自己的便罢。"名者,实之宾也",不关什么紧要的。

Transient and Death-Is-Predestined. If you say they are, in appearance they are different. Thus in Picture A on the fourth page of illustrations, Wu Chang of the world of men is not wearing a gaudy robe and gauze headdress; but Wu Chang of the shades is rather similar to Death-Is-Predestined in the other picture, although he has no abacus and is holding a fan. Of course we can say this was probably in summer, but in that case why has he grown such a bushy beard? Is it because plague is so rife in summer that he is too busy to have time even for a shave? This picture comes, I may say, from the Siguozhai edition printed in Tianjin. And those in the Peking and Guangzhou editions are similar.

Picture B is from the Liguangmingzhuang edition printed in Nanjing. Its Wu Changs are like those in Picture A, but their names are interchanged. What the Tianjin edition calls Wu Chang of the shades is named Wu Chang of the world of men in the Nanjing edition. Still, this coincides with my own view. So provided there is a figure dressed in white with a tall hat, whether bearded or not, people in Peking, Tianjin and Guangzhou may call him Wu Chang of the shades or Death-Is-Predestined, but I and the people of Nanjing call him Life-Is-Transient, each giving him whatevername we please. After all, "The name is just an attribute of the fact." Hence what we call him does not matter much.

不过我还要添上一点C图，是绍兴许广记刻本中的一部分，上面并无题字，不知宣传者于意云何。我幼小时常常走过许广记的门前，也闲看他们刻图画，是专爱用弧线和直线，不大肯作曲线的，所以无常先生的真相，在这里也难以判然。只是他身边另有一个小高帽，却还能分明看出，为别的本子上所无。这就是我所说过的在赛会时候出现的阿领。他连办公时间也带着儿子(?)走，我想，大概是在叫他跟随学习，预备长大之后，可以“无改于父之道”的。

除勾摄人魂外，十殿阎罗王中第四殿五官王的案桌旁边，也什九站着一个高帽脚色。如D图，1取自天津的思过斋本，模样颇漂亮；2是南京本，舌头拖出来了，不知何故；3是广州的宝经阁本，扇子破了；4是北京龙光斋本，无扇，下巴之下一条黑，我看不透它是胡子还是舌头；5是天津石印局本，也颇漂亮，然而站到第七殿泰山王的公案桌过去

Still, I decided to add Picture C from the Xuguangji edition of Shaoxing. As it has no caption, I don't know the artist's intention. When I was small I used to pass that printing shop and sometimes watched them engraving these pictures. As they preferred to draw circles and straight lines, seldom curved lines, from their version it is hard to judge the true appearance of Mr. Wu Chang. Beside him, however, we can see quite clearly another little tall-hat who is absent from other editions. This must be the Ah-ling who appears during temple fairs, as I mentioned before. So even when performing official duties he brings along his son(?). I suppose he wants the child to learn from him, in order that when grown up he "will not change his father's ways."

Apart from the Summoner of Spirits, beside the desk of the King of Wuguan of the Fourth Court among the ten Kings of Hell, there usually stands a figure in a tall hat like that in Picture D, No. 1, from the Siguozhai edition of Tianjin, who looks quite elegant. NO.2, from the Nanjing edition, for some reason is sticking out his tongue. No. 3, from the Baojingge edition of Guangzhou, has a broken fan. No.4, from the Longguangzhai edition of Peking, has no fan, and under his chin is a black line which may be a beard ortongue for all I know. No. 5, from the Lithographic Printing Shop edition of Tianjin, also looks quite elegant; but he is standing by the desk of the King of Taishan of the Seventh

了:这是很特别的。

又,老虎噬人的图上,也一定画有一个高帽的脚色,拿着纸扇子暗地里在指挥。不知道这也就是无常呢,还是所谓"伥鬼"?但我乡戏文上的伥鬼都不戴高帽子。

研究这一类三魂渺渺,七魄茫茫,"死无对证"的学问,是很新颖,也极占便宜的。假使征集材料,开始讨论,将各种往来的信件都编印起来,恐怕也可以出三四本颇厚的书,并且因此升为"学者"。但是,"活无常学者",名称不大冠冕,我不想干下去了,只在这里下一个武断:——

《玉历》式的思想是很粗浅的:"活无常"和"死有分",合起来是人生的象征。大将死时,本只须死有分来到。因为他一到,这时候,也就可见"活无常"。

但民间又有一种自称"走阴"或"阴

Court instead, which is rather unusual.

Again, in pictures of tigers eating men, there is always a character in a tall hat, holding a paper fan to give the tiger secret directions. I don't know whether this is also Wu Chang or the ghost known as "Chang" (伥). However, in the operas in my home district, the "Chang" ghost does not wear a tall hat.

Researches into such esoteric matters as the lore of spirits and the supernatural, not being verifiable by facts, are most original and highly advantageous too. If I put all the materials together, started a scholarly discussion, and compiled and printed all the correspondence of different sorts received, I dare say I could produce three or four massive volumes and by so doing rise to the rank of a "scholar." Still, the title "Wu-chang-ologist" lacks distinction, so I have no wish to pursue my researches further and will simply conclude here in arbitrary fashion:

The ideas in such books as the *Jade Calendar* are very crude and simple: Life-Is-Transient and Death-Is-Predestined together symbolize the life of man. When a man is about to die only Death-Is-Predestined need turn up, for his arrival shows that "life is transient."

Among the people, however, is also a type of self-styled "messenger for the nether regions," liv-

差”的，是生人暂时入冥，帮办公事的脚色。因为他帮同勾魂摄魄，大家也就称之为“无常”；又以其本是生魂也，则别之曰“阳”，但从此便和“活无常”隐然相混了。如第四图版之 A，题为“阳无常”的，是平常人的普通装束，足见明明是阴差，他的职务只在领鬼卒进门，所以站在阶下。

既有了生魂入冥的“阳无常”，便以“阴无常”来称职务相似而并非生魂的死有分了。

做目连戏和迎神赛会虽说是祷祈，同时也等于娱乐，扮演出来的应该是阴差，而普通状态太无趣，——无所谓扮演，——不如奇特些好，于是就将“那一个无常”的衣装给他穿上了；——自然原也没有知道得很清楚。然而从此也更传讹下去。所以南京人和我之所谓活无常，是阴差而穿着死有分的衣冠，

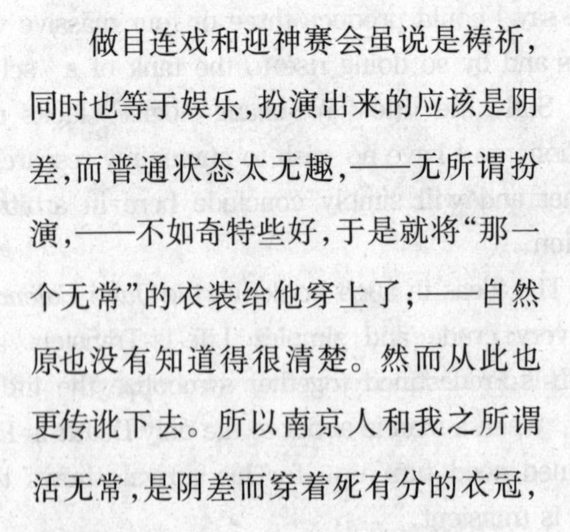

ing men who go for a time to the shades to help carry our official tasks. Because they help to summon spirits, people call them Wu Chang too; and because they are the spirits of living men they are designated as belonging to the world of men, and so become confused with Life-Is-Transient. Thus Picture A in the fourth page of illustrations shows Wu Chang of the world of men dressed in ordinary human costume to indicate that he is just a messenger to the shades, whose job is only to guide the ghost guard to the house. This is why he is standing at the foot of the steps.

Since there is a Wu Chang who is a living man's spirit who goes to the nether regions, Death-Is-Predestined is known as Wu Chang of the shades, as he has similar tasks but is not of the world of men.

Though the Mandgalyayana dramas and temple processions were designed to appease the gods, they serve as entertainment too. If the character playing the part of the live messenger to the shades were to dress as an ordinary man it would look too uninteresting, for then it would not be a masquerade. It is better to make him more bizarre-looking. This is why he is dressed in the costume of the other Wu Chang — of course, what this is people never knew too clearly. And in this way the mistake was perpetuated. So what people in Nanjing and I call Life-Is-Transient is really the livingmessenger to

顶着真的活无常的名号，大背经典，荒谬得很的。

不知海内博雅君子，以为如何？

我本来并不准备做什么后记，只想寻几张旧画像来做插图，不料目的不达，便变成一面比较，剪贴，一面乱发议论了。那一点本文或作或辍地几乎做了一年，这一点后记也或作或辍地几乎做了两个月。天热如此，汗流浃背，是亦不可以已乎：爰为结。

一九二七年七月十一日，写完于广州东堤寓楼之西窗下。

the shades wearing the costume of Death-Is-Predestined while using the name Life-Is-Transient. This is utterly counter to classical lore and most preposterous.

Would the erudite gentlemen of China agree with my conclusions?

I had no intention at first of writing a postscript. I just wanted to find a few old pictures as illustrations and didn't expect to get off the track. While making comparisons of the pictures, cutting out and pasting together specimens, I have made my random comments. The text or the reminiscences has taken me about a year off and on, while this brief postscript too has taken me nearly two months off and on. It is so hot that sweat is pouring down my back. High time, surely, to make an end of it? With this I conclude.

Written by the west window of my lodging
At Dongdi, Guangzhou
July 11, 1927